You, Your Family and the Internet

What every Christian in the digital age ought to know

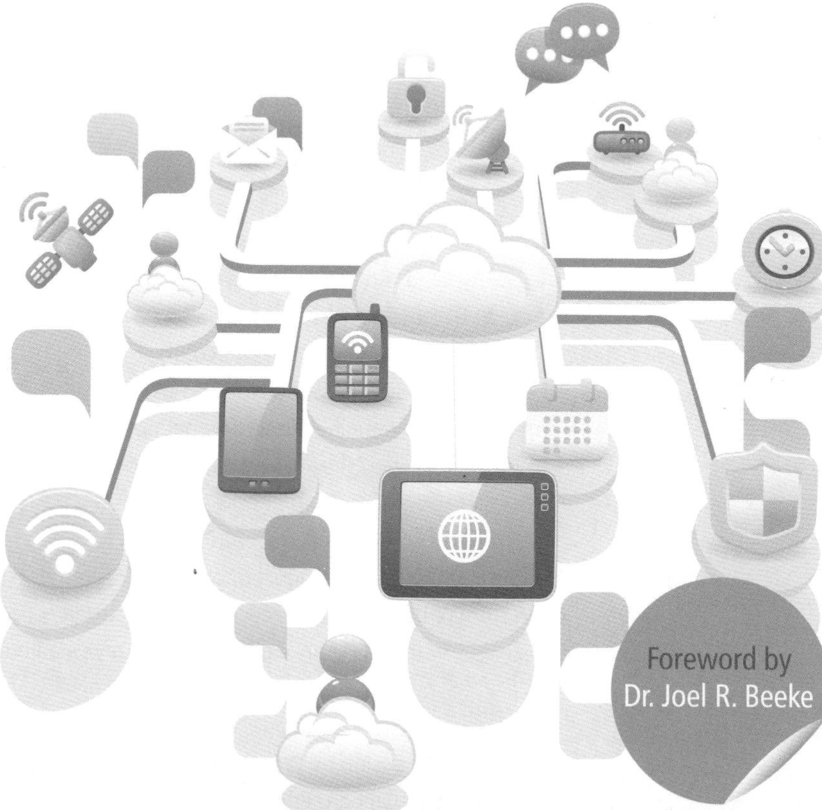

DayOne

Foreword by Dr. Joel R. Beeke

David Clark

The unique strength of David Clark's contribution is in his application of key biblical principles.—Tim Challies

© Day One Publications 2012
First printed 2012

ISBN 978-1-84625-340-9

British Library Cataloguing in Publication Data available

Unless otherwise indicated, Scripture quotations are from the **New King James Version (NKJV)**®. Copyright © 1982 by Thomas Nelson, Inc. Used by permission. All rights reserved.

Published by Day One Publications
Ryelands Road, Leominster, HR6 8NZ
☎ 01568 613 740 FAX 01568 611 473
email—sales@dayone.co.uk
web site—www.dayone.co.uk
North American—e-mail—sales@dayonebookstore.com
North American—web site—www.dayonebookstore.com

All rights reserved
No part of this publication may be reproduced, or stored in a retrieval system, or transmitted, in any form or by any means, mechanical, electronic, photocopying, recording or otherwise, without the prior permission of Day One Publications.

Cover design by Wayne McMaster
Printed by Orchard Press Cheltenham Ltd

Commendations

Today some two billion people around the world use the Internet. Almost 80% of North Americans are connected to the web. But even as we use it, few of us understand the dizzying array of its applications and implications. David Clark guides us through the complexities of the Internet with simple, clear explanations. Even better, he unveils the spiritual implications of the Internet, both positive and negative. Pastors, parents, and teachers will greatly appreciate this book, as will the everyday Christian who, like me, is struggling to keep up with the ever-expanding universe of cyber-space, desiring to use it to God's glory and the welfare of our families and Christ's church.

—Dr. Joel R. Beeke, President, Puritan Reformed Theological Seminary, Grand Rapids, Michigan

Much has been written about living as Christians in this digital world; much more will be written in the days and years to come. The unique strength of David Clark's contribution is in his application of key biblical principles that will guide our use of these technologies and inform our dedication to them.

—Tim Challies, Author and Blogger, Ontario, Canada

This excellent little book should be in every Christian home. Christians would also do well to share copies with their unbelieving friends. David Clark masterfully takes us through the various aspects of the bewildering world of Internet technology, shows the dangers associated with each, and gives commonsense advice for avoiding those dangers. His 'Five Principles to Learn From' and 'Five Principles to Run With' (chapters 11 and 12) provide extremely valuable ways for Christians to get a handle on the Internet.

—Roger Ellsworth, Pastor with an itinerant ministry, and author of over thirty books

If you or your children use the Internet, buy and use this book! David Clark combines his expert technical knowledge of the field with a sensitive use of biblical principles to help us navigate the pitfalls and garner the benefits of the technology which we use every day. The result is a skilful blend of useful information and wise Christian counsel.

—Robert Strivens, Principal, London Theological Seminary

Commendations

You, Your Family and the Internet, written by David Clark, is an excellent book. This is a must-read for every Christian; it is a must-read for every parent, and it should be read by every teenager who is being bombarded by the technology of the internet and the mass media. I have reviewed this book, and as a pastor will have my entire congregation read this as a part of their discipleship and Christian growth. Although this book is informative, practical, and encouraging, it also serves as a warning of the dangers that lurk in the murky modern world of computers and the Internet. David Clark points out the many benefits and blessings of the internet, but also educates his readers of the realities of its dangers. The book discusses such topics as internet browsing, Facebook, Twitter, internet games and many other relevant subjects. I highly recommend this book as a helpful tool for parents and pastors alike to enable them to disciple their families and their churches.

—Bob Dickie, author and pastor

It is true that the Internet has brought all the world into our homes. This includes good and evil, beauty and ugliness, truth and falsehood. How are Christian parents to deal with this onslaught on our homes and our children? David Clark has provided a much-needed service to the church by writing a book on this very issue. He takes a very balanced approach, and one that is needed in the church. I can't think of a more pressing issue for the church to deal with. I encourage every parent to buy this book and to work through it diligently. Do not be caught unawares!

—John D. Currid, Carl McMurray Professor of Old Testament, Reformed Theological Seminary-Charlotte

About the Author

David Clark was born and brought up in a missionary family working in France. A Bible-believing Christian since the age of fifteen, he is active in his local Evangelical and Reformed church in England, where he lives after spending a number of years in the USA.

He has worked with computer technologies for over thirty years, has a degree in Computer Science and Electronics, and has carried out postgraduate research into the uses of Artificial Intelligence in the design of silicon chips. He owns and runs a consulting company that carries out technology-related work for the UK and US governments. He has published a number of technical papers at various conferences, ranging from the use of Artificial Intelligence to Risk Analysis. He has also served on the boards of *Evangelical Times* and *Evangelical Press*, as well as working in publishing in the Russian and Chinese languages. He is on the editorial committee for *Christian Hymns*. He is married with two children and has recently become a grandfather.

Acknowledgements

This book had its origin in a series of articles published in the UK, USA and Brazil. For this I own thanks to a large number of people, particularly Roger Fay of *Evangelical Times*, John Benton of *Evangelicals Now*, Joel Beeke who published the original articles in the *Banner of Sovereign Grace Truth*, Kent Philpott from *Earthen Vessel Publishing*, Jim Holmes of *Day One Publications* and friends at *FIEL* in Brazil who painstakingly translated the articles into Portuguese. A special thanks should also go to all those dear friends who took the time to read and comment on the manuscript as it went through its various alterations, particularly Jonathan Pountney. Finally, I owe an untold debt of gratitude to my long-suffering wife Carolyn, without whom none of this would have been possible.

May God, in his infinite goodness and mercy, be pleased to use this short book to glorify his name and build up his church.

Be sober, be vigilant; because your adversary the devil walks about like a roaring lion, seeking whom he may devour. Resist him, steadfast in the faith, knowing that the same sufferings are experienced by your brotherhood in the world. But may the God of all grace, who called us to His eternal glory by Christ Jesus, after you have suffered a while, perfect, establish, strengthen, and settle you. (1 Peter 5:8–10)

Further Resources

For further resources, comments and updates see www.theInternet.me or select the QR code below.

Dedication

Dedication

This book is dedicated to my children, Sarah and Tim.

Contents

FOREWORD	10
1 INTRODUCTION	12
2 SO WHAT?	15
3 THE BAD, THE GOOD AND A DOSE OF HISTORY	24
4 COMMUNICATION	31
5 FACEBOOK AND THE SOCIAL NETWORK REVOLUTION	38
6 PORNOGRAPHY	48
7 IF IT'S FREE, THEN YOU ARE THE PRODUCT…	57
8 INTERNET GAMES	66
9 INTERNET GAMBLING	75
10 NEWS AND VIEWS	82
11 FIVE PRINCIPLES TO LEARN FROM	90
12 FIVE PRINCIPLES TO RUN WITH	100

Foreword

Fifty years ago, if someone told you to grab a mouse, point it, and double-click it to tweet, you might have been accused of cruelty to animals. Today, information technology pervades our lives. Nowhere is this truer than in the rapidly expanding cyber-world of the Internet.

We ignore the Internet to our own peril. Like any form of technology, it has great potential for good as well as evil. Parents must know how to guide their children through its numerous options. Teachers must understand how students can use the Internet, whether for research or for cheating. Pastors should be equipped with a basic understanding of its operations so that they can broadcast the gospel to all nations and protect their congregations from its corruptions. We all should get a grip on this powerful tool to use it for the glory of God.

David Clark is well equipped to explain such matters. He has been working with the Internet for three decades, since studying computer science at college. In clear and simple language, Clark explains the ways in which the Internet is determining how people communicate and form communities, sell products and analyze trends, play online games and gamble away their money, view distant friends and destroy their souls with pornography, share the news, and make the news by mobilizing mass movements quickly.

But this book does more than just educate us about technology. Clark also charts a course for Christians through the dangers, delusions, and opportunities of the Internet. He shows us that the Internet not only opens a door for us to access information and images but also provides others with information about us and our lives. He warns us of the false sense of privacy and freedom that Internet users feel, while their actions may lead to very public consequences.

Repeatedly, he calls us to exercise wisdom and self-control in using the Internet. This is our calling in every age. God's grace teaches us that "denying ungodliness and worldly lusts, we should live soberly, righteously, and godly in this present age" (Titus 2:12). That doesn't just mean we must avoid bad websites. It commands us to redeem the time for God (Ephesians 5:16). May God use this book to keep our salt salty, and to shine our light brightly until every nation glorifies our Father.

Joel R. Beeke
President, Puritan Reformed Theological Seminary
Grand Rapids, Michigan

Chapter 1

Introduction

This book is written by a Christian, for Christians. It is also written for anyone who has felt the impact of the Internet in his or her day-to-day life. It is probably fair to say that almost every human being living on the planet today now falls into this category, whether directly or indirectly.

Whether we are parents, grandparents, church officers or members, most of us have wondered how to grapple with the impact of the Internet in our lives and those of others.

While many look to the Bible for guidance, nowhere will we find in it any reference to the Internet. Moses did not use an iPad. The apostle Paul did not post a blog. The early church did not use Facebook to organize events. All Scripture—both the Old Testament as well as the New Testament—was written before the printed page, the age of steam, electricity, electronics, robotics, cars, aircraft and all the many innovations that have revolutionized the way that we live and interact with one another.

Does the Bible really have nothing to say to us today? My contention in this book is that there is nothing more important than studying and applying the Word of God if we are to understand how to live today. Nothing has fundamentally changed with who we are; our nature; our essential being. The Bible is full of vital principles that can be effectively applied to the way that we live, both today and throughout time. The problem is not with the Bible being out of date, but rather with our unwillingness to think about how to apply principles such as self-control, accountability and good stewardship of our time.

Since biblical principles are timeless, these can be applied effectively even when modern technologies seem to change every few months. Because of this, this book is not a prescriptive "how to" book. Though many may be helped by such books, I have always found them infuriating, with their assumption that if the reader follows the prescribed recipe, then all will work out. Rather, the purpose of this book is to help you think through how best to use the Internet in your own unique situation.

Introduction

Nor is this book philosophical or polemic. It is not my goal to foster a really good debate, as interesting as this may be. Neither is the goal to predict how the Internet will evolve or where the next big idea will come from. In my thirty years of working in this area, the one thing I can consistently say is that almost every prediction has been wrong. Other books have sought to grapple with these issues, such as the recent book from Tim Challies[1] in which he sets out to explore the tensions between the theory of technology, theology and experience.

This book is first and foremost practical. I have sought to identify key Internet technologies, explain them, explore how they affect our lives, and draw out biblical principles that can be applied to how we deal with issues associated with these technologies, particularly in our interactions with others, our churches and our families. I am a Christian, and the whole of this book is based on what are called "Judeo-Christian values'"—the same basic values that we still find underpinning many democracies and that are effectively derived from the Bible.

Based on these values, we will draw out principles that are timeless, wise and that can then be brought to bear on the way we deal with the impact of Internet technologies.

In the first two chapters, we will lay some basic groundwork. After these, we will look at a series of technologies and then, finally, conclude with a summary of the key principles and some of the opportunities that lie ahead of us.

You will also find questions for discussion at the end of many chapters. My hope is that you will use these perhaps in adult Bible classes, youth groups or book discussions to explore and think further about the subjects presented in the chapter. So that discussions are focused correctly, you will find a number of Scripture references. May I urge you to read these first, before venturing opinions, so that discussion is based first and foremost on what God has to say to us.

It is easy to become a scaremonger about Internet technologies; it is much harder to look at these objectively, avoid the very real dangers, and, at the same time, make the most of the amazing opportunities in a wise and productive manner. This is the goal of this book. If in some small way I have succeeded, my prayer is that you will be renewed in your

Chapter 1

zeal to serve and worship the Lord Jesus Christ, who is sovereign over all and holds everything together by his powerful word (Hebrews 1:3) because one day we will have to give an account for the opportunities he gave us (Luke 12:48). Let us not waste them!

Note

1 **Challies, T.,** *The Next Story* (Zondervan, 2011)

So What?

As I write this text, our first grandchild, Evie, has just been born to our daughter and son-in-law. Not only am I an immensely proud and happy grandparent, but, within a few hours, the news of Evie's birth had reached four continents, with congratulatory notes appearing on Facebook along with pictures of the beaming, but tired, parents holding their firstborn. By the end of the day, hundreds of people knew about her birth, with notes, emails, postings and text messages being received from across the world.

It does not seem that long ago that our son and daughter were born. Back then, just over twenty years ago, things were not so instant. Yes, there were phone calls to inform the happy grandparents, and the waiting family. But beyond that, news would have trickled out over days and weeks. Very few people were on email, there was no Facebook, no texting, no Skype, no IM, no tweets from the delivery room. How things have changed … or have they?

So What Has Changed?

In terms of raw technology, little has changed in the last fifty or sixty years. In the developed world, most homes have a number of electrical, mechanical and electronic devices that are all supposedly there to make life more convenient, or provide in-home entertainment. Most of these are not recent inventions. Consider, for example, the humble refrigerator. It may surprise you to learn that in 1873 a German inventor by the name of Carl Von Linde demonstrated the first practical and portable compressor refrigeration machine in Munich. A similar thing can be said of the washing machine with the "Thor" electric powered washing machine first being introduced in 1908 by the Hurley Machine Company of Chicago, Illinois.

Prior to the Internet, no device had a bigger impact in the second half of the twentieth century than the television, although it was first introduced in 1928, with the first color television being demonstrated in 1938. The car (1886), aircraft (1903) and train (1807) all have long and distinguished histories.

Chapter 2

What of items that we consider more modern? Take, for example, the computer. There is debate over what constitutes the first computer. Some say that the credit should go to the Frenchman Joseph Marie Jacquard who, in 1801 invented the Jacquard loom, a mechanical textile loom that was controlled by punched cards.

Others suggest that the English mathematician Charles Babbage is the true father of modern computing. Babbage was concerned about removing human error in calculating logarithmic tables. Interestingly, the people who calculated these tables by hand were called "computers"—someone who computes. In 1822 Babbage began work on what he called the difference engine. This project was never completed during Babbage's lifetime, though parts of the original difference engine

ENIAC—the first digital computer. It had the equivalent of 1,800 transistors.

So What?

can be seen at the London Science Museum. In 1991 a difference engine was built using Babbage's original plans and it worked!

Some would contend that the first digital computer, the Colossus, was built by British engineers and mathematicians in secret during the second world war to crack the German encryption code. For others, the first digital computer, the "Electronic Numerical Integrator And Computer" or ENIAC[1] for short, was built in 1946 at the University of Pennsylvania to calculate artillery firing tables for the United States Army's Ballistic Research Laboratory. It weighed 27 tons, took up 680 square feet and used so much power (150 kW) that all the lights in the neighborhood would dim when it was switched on.

Even the mobile phone, perhaps the most pervasive device of the twenty-first century with nearly 5 billion phone subscriptions by the end of the first decade,[2] was invented in 1973 by Dr. Martin Cooper. It may have looked more like a very large brick, but it was still portable and capable of making phone calls.

The truth of the matter is that the appliances and gadgets that we use would, for the most part, have been available thirty or forty years ago, and that most of what we use in the home or as a mode of transportation dates back nearly a hundred years, and sometimes more. So much for our modern society!

What Is The Fuss All About?

But something has changed, and changed so fundamentally that it can be likened to the impact of the Industrial Revolution that took place at the close of the eighteenth and into the nineteenth century. Now, as then, society changed in deep and indelible ways, ways that meant that our world would never be the same again.

Two economists, writing in a book entitled *Elementary Principles of Economics*,[3] explain how the Industrial Revolution led to changes in agriculture, manufacture, transportation, and even economic legislation and labor laws. The changes had a profound effect on the country, with people moving into cities, and the growth of national and international markets that simply did not exist before.

In other words, while the Industrial Revolution ushered in many new

Chapter 2

technologies, its greatest impact was the way that it changed how society works, and the way that people interact and live. Another commentator puts it this way: "Changes in agriculture, manufacturing, mining, transportation, and technology had a profound effect on the socioeconomic and cultural conditions of the times."4

These are the very same kinds of changes that we are experiencing as a result of the Internet revolution. The major impacts of our current technological revolution come not so much from new technology or the latest gadgets but, as with the Industrial Revolution, are found in the way that people interact and live. This affects the very fabric of our society and how we relate to civil, public and religious institutions. They impact the friends that we make, what we care about, and the kind of family life we have. Clay Shirky, a professor at New York University writing in the British *Guardian* newspaper, likens the impact of the Internet to that of the printing press: "The era when a small set of professionals controlled media creation is over. Anyone can now say anything to anyone. Make no mistake, the web is the biggest media revolution since the printing press."5

The World In Miniature

There is no doubt that technological developments in the second half of the twentieth century have formed the basis for the changes. In 1959, two engineers, Jack Kirby (who also invented the portable calculator) and Robert Noyce (who went on to found Intel), separately filed patents on ways to pack transistors and other electronic components onto an integrated circuit (or chip as it later became known). From modest beginnings, these chips have grown to hold over 700 million transistors. Throughout the last fifty years, the power of these chips has steadily increased, so much so that there is hardly any modern appliance that does not extensively use such technology. Our whole Western society relies on these chips, whether in computers, telephones, GPS devices, satellites, or, in fact, just about everything we use from day to day.

For example, imagine buying some apples at a local store. The farmer will certainly have kept a close eye on the weather—with forecasts delivered courtesy of huge super computers. There would have been

So What?

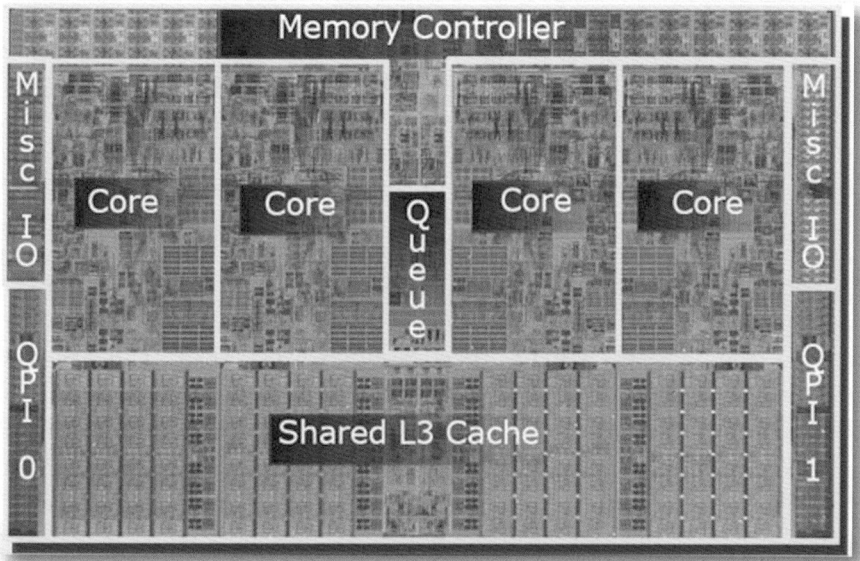

Intel's I7 Processor, with 731 million transistors

chips controlling the tractors used in farming (and not to mention the business side of the enterprise that would have relied on phone, fax and computer—all containing chips). Once the apples were picked and packed, they would have been transported to a distribution facility—all controlled with computers, the shipping and trucking almost certainly recorded and tracked using GPS tags, and the containers kept at a constant temperature with a control system—all of these contain and use chips. When they finally arrive at the local supermarket, they are inventoried (with computers), displayed in a temperature-controlled case, and scanned at the register by the checkout assistant—all using computer technology to work. Satisfied with our apple purchase, we drive home in our car (which also uses microchips that constantly control and record details) and place these in our computer-controlled refrigerator. Try doing that without the microchip!

Not only are microchips everywhere, but the number of transistors that can be packed onto these chips doubles about every two years.[6] This has led to a remarkable increase in computational power as well as an

Chapter 2

amazing decrease in device sizes. Today, a smart phone[7] is around 30,000 times more powerful than the first digital computer, while a top-end laptop can process information 1,500,000 times faster. All of this is the result of some amazing miniaturization.

Some scientists have gone even further and see computers and robots becoming as intelligent as people by the year 2045. They call it the "singularity". One of the key proponents of this concept, an Massachusetts Institute of Technology professor by the name of Kurzweil, explains[8] that "computers are not only getting faster, they are getting faster faster"—if the speed doubles every year, then just like compound interest the speed increases at a higher and higher rate. The term "singularity" was first used in 1965 by a British mathematician named I.J. Good to describe something he called an "intelligence explosion". Kurzweil explains that when he extended the rates at which various technologies have been improving into the future, this is what he found: "We will successfully reverse-engineer the human brain by the mid-2020s. By the end of that decade, computers will be capable of human-level intelligence". In 2045 he estimates that, "given the vast increases in computing power and the vast reductions in the cost of the same, the quantity of artificial intelligence created will be about a billion times the sum of all the human intelligence that exists today".

These are outlandish claims, and I strongly disagree with them. What makes us human and different from animals is first and foremost our soul, then a host of other attributes, be they our capacity to love, hate, create, destroy, worship or even debate over the very existence of a creating God. The same applies to inanimate computer programs, which will never be capable of feeling, loving, or any other human emotion, let alone have a soul.

The World Is Personal

We began this chapter by suggesting that we have undergone a cataclysmic change in our society, particularly in the way that we relate to one another. It is not an exaggeration to suggest that the Internet has become an indispensable part of modern business life. Not only is it a business tool, but the Internet now reaches many homes across the world. In Europe, 390 million people have access to the Internet in their homes—roughly half of the population.[9] In the UK, that number rises to nearly 71% of households, and 74% in North America. Across the world, an estimated 1 billion people now have access to the Internet.[10] Put differently, something close to one seventh of the world's population has access to anything that is posted on a web page.

What has made the difference is not just miniaturization, but personalization. Technology is not only available but it is there in our homes and our workplaces. The technologies that have been the most successful, and the ones that are still shaping the kind of world we live in, are the ones that increase our sense of self-worth, and play to some of the most innate senses that lie at the center of the "me" generation.

In their influential book on macroeconomics,[11] authors Akerlof and Shiller suggest that what drives our economies is not so much rational behavior, such as a reasoned response for supply and demand or the threat of inflation, but rather what they term "animal spirits", and what we might call base human responses such as group panic, selfishness, greed and self-interest. These are the same responses that drive which technologies succeed and which do not. In their book, they postulate that one of the important economic drivers are stories, which, to date, have been promulgated (or even at times invented!) by the traditional media—television and print. They explain that "we might model the spread of a story in terms of an epidemic. Stories are like viruses." What we have seen when events in the Middle East led to widespread unrest and the downfall of several governments, with technologies like Twitter and Facebook, is that those "viruses" now spread through the Internet, no longer from mass-media to the people, but in a personal way, from one person directly to another. Our communications have become very personal, with the Internet in general and social media in particular being the conduit of information. We are all linked and intertwined in a way that was never possible before. Like a Tsunami as the sea level rises, we all rise with it. We are driven along by the flow of interconnected humankind.

We live in what has been termed a postmodern society where we can all believe different things without fear of contradicting each other. What matters is what it means to "me", and it is just fine if something means

Chapter 2

something different to you. In other words, the individual is the center of the universe, and the whole world revolves around it. Whether we agree with this viewpoint or not, if we are honest, we will discover that we have all been contaminated by this view of life—however little we care to admit it. There is nothing new here, as it plays on some of the more basic human traits—self-centeredness, selfishness, lack of self-control, and so on.

The really successful technologies are those that have reinforced some of these societal trends. Who would have foreseen the rise of the mobile phone? The selling point is that it makes us feel so important that we need to be available all of the time ... just in case? Or why the need to let people know what we are doing all of the time (on Facebook) or count the number of Twitter followers? Who cares what we had for breakfast, or whether the cat next door is stopping us from sleeping? But in today's society, we now find that we have insurmountable urges to share this with our friends. Why?

Whether it be a laptop (or personal computer), or the Smartphone (that we seem to have to carry all the time), or Facebook, Twitter or Groupons, these are all shaping the kind of world we live in. We have information available all of the time—we can Google anything, we are accessible all of the time, we know what our friends are doing, where they are and share in their every experience—instantly. The world is both highly personal and strangely impersonal at the same time.

As we shall see in this book, the impact of the Internet is not always a bad thing, but the dangers need to be recognized and controlled, particularly in our churches and families.

Notes

1. Picture of ENIAC from Wikipedia, taken by unidentified U.S. Army photographer. This work is in the public domain in the United States because it is a work of the United States Federal Government under the terms of Title 17, Chapter 1, Section 105 of the US Code.
2. From a CBS News report:
    www.cbsnews.com/stories/2010/02/15/business/main6209772.shtml
3. **Richard Theodore Ely, George Ray Wicker,** *Elementary Principles Of Economics: Together With A Short Sketch Of Economic History* (Kessinger Publishing LLC, 2007)

So What?

4 Quoted from the Wikipedia article on the Industrial Revolution: en.wikipedia.org/wiki/Industrial_Revolution
5 *The Guardian,* Monday 18 May 2009
6 The co-founder of Intel, Gordon E Moore, first postulated that the number of transistors would double every two years in the 1970s. Remarkably, he has been proved right so far, leading to this statement becoming known as "Moore's law".
7 The computational power is measured in Millions of Instructions Per Second—MIPS. The first digital computer, the ENIAC, was capable of 0.05 MIPS, or 50,000 instructions per second. An iPhone can perform at about 1500 MIPS. Today's Intel Core i7 Extreme 965EE can perform about 80,000 MIPS.
8 From a *Time Magazine* article Feb. 10, 2011
9 www.internetworldstats.com/stats.htm
10 news.yahoo.com/s/ap/20090831/ap_on_bi_ge/us_tec_internet_at40
11 **George A. Akerlof** and **Robert J. Shiller,** *Animal Spirits: How Human Psychology Drives the Economy, and Why It Matters for Global Capitalism* (Princeton University Press, 2009)

Chapter 3

The Bad, the Good, and a Dose of History

In March 2008, British psychologist Dr. Tanya Byron published the result of a government-commissioned study (the Byron Report) that was tasked to "undertake a review of the evidence on risks to children's safety and wellbeing of exposure to potentially harmful or inappropriate material on the internet ... and to make recommendations for improvements or additional action."[1] The report concluded that "the Internet cannot be made completely safe."[2]

The Bad

In 2006 there were over 4 million pornography websites, 100,000 of which offered illegal child pornography.[3] A survey carried out for a British newspaper[4] revealed that 66% of women have watched porn, while nearly nine out of ten men (88%) fit that category, with a quarter of them watching it every day. The popular American magazine *Christianity Today* suggested that "seventy percent of American men ages 18–34 view Internet pornography once a month."[5] The same article went on to explain that churches are not immune to the problem "One evangelical leader was skeptical of survey findings that said 50 percent of Christian men have looked at porn recently. So he surveyed his own congregation. He found that 60 percent had done so within the past year, and 25 percent within the past 30 days".

Time Magazine, in an article entitled "Adultery 2.0" explained that there are now websites developed with slick applications (apps) for the iPhone, Android and the Blackberry aimed at "tech savvy adulterers wary of leaving tracks on work or home computers". "Cheating has never been easier," is the claim of AshleyMadison.com, a personals site designed to facilitate extramarital affairs.[6]

The list goes on, with repeated warnings to be wary of Internet crime, identity theft and pedophiles among others. It is hardly surprising that most parents wonder if the social networks their children spend so much time using are safe. Or if they should even let their children use mobile phones, given police warnings concerning the practice of "sexting" in which young people send explicit and indecent photos to each other using their mobile phones.[7]

What should we do? How do parents cope with these problems when there is such a gap between the young Internet-savvy generation and the majority of parents?

In this chapter we will take a high-level look at the issues involved, while in subsequent chapters we will explore key areas, such as social networks, Internet addiction, virtual relationships, gambling, pornography, blogging, and others. These things are shaping the lives of many around us, and we need to know both what is happening and how to deal with the issues in our families, relationships, society, church, and culture.

The Good

Yes, there is also good and we should not forget about it. The Internet has created untold opportunities for people to interact across the world, whether they are presenting Christianity or receiving help from the thousands of support groups available online. As a Christian, I am excited at the idea that we can now bring the gospel of Jesus Christ to 2 billion people, all without leaving our office or home. One well-known pastor and public speaker ably captured some of this when he commented that "the Internet has opened an opportunity for an entirely new way of communicating the gospel of Jesus Christ to the nations of the earth."[8]

Hymns, multiple versions of the Bible, and articles on just about every conceivable theological topic are all available at the click of a button. For example, while preparing this book, I was directed in the Day One Publications house style to use the latest Bible editions "found online at www.biblegateway.com". We can sit at a computer and find out about almost any church or Christian organization anywhere in the world. Missionaries, charities and para-church organizations have been able to drastically cut their costs by using emails, websites and social networks to communicate with their supporters. An Evangelical conservative website, www.sermonaudio.com, boasts thousands of sermons from MacArthur to Spurgeon, with hundreds being added every week. There are blogs, discussion forums, videos and courses online. We can tweet with others, create Facebook events, or talk face to face using a video webcam with a friend or missionary anywhere in the world. At its heart, the Internet is a communications tool, and Christians everywhere are using it to communicate the wonderful truths of Jesus Christ.

The Internet has also opened up a myriad of other helpful opportunities. For example, there are hosts of support groups available online for just about every situation or condition. Reporting on the impact of the Internet for people with rare diseases, US commentator Nancy Shute explained on National Public Radio that "it can be hard to find expert medical advice, especially in the midst of a medical crisis... The Web has been a game-changer for those people, connecting them to others in the same boat. They share medical information and support each other on list-servers, chat rooms, and now Facebook."[9]

What is the Internet?

Before we go much further, we must attempt to demystify the Internet. At its core, it is very simple (though, of course, there are a lot of complex technologies supporting it). Much like the printed page, it is at its heart a communications tool.

The Internet can be likened to the postal system. Imagine that we write and send a letter, or, worse, receive a bill. In either case, someone has put a piece of paper in an envelope, addressed it, and the postal system has delivered it to an appropriate mailbox. Now, suppose for instance that we wanted to buy a new shirt from a company located somewhere in the country. We could write them a letter giving them some information about size and preferences. In return they may mail out a photograph of one of their shirts and some cost information. Perhaps, when we take a look at the picture, we decide that we do not like the look of that particular shirt and write back to them asking for another type of shirt. In response, they might send a picture of a different shirt, and so on.

The Bad, the Good, and a Dose of History

Clearly, using the postal system in this way would be extremely slow and inefficient. This is why most companies would simply send out a catalogue with all their products in it. However, the example illustrates how the Internet works. Without going into technical details, suffice it to say that every computer has an individual address—just like the postal system. The Internet acts like an electronic version of the postal service, delivering information a page at a time. It's just much, much faster. The pages (or other information such as sound or video streams) are held on a web server and delivered according to what each user requests—typically the pages are navigated using search parameters or links (called hyperlinks) that can be "clicked" on the computer screen. It is the speed and ease of use that has created such a pervasive network of interconnected computers, companies and people.

How Did It Happen?

On September 2, 2009, the Internet turned forty.[10] However, as this graph[11] clearly shows, it is likely that many people started using it no more than ten years ago. While to a teenager, ten years may seem a long time, to most of us, ten years or even forty years is not really that long. I first came across the Internet some thirty years ago while studying

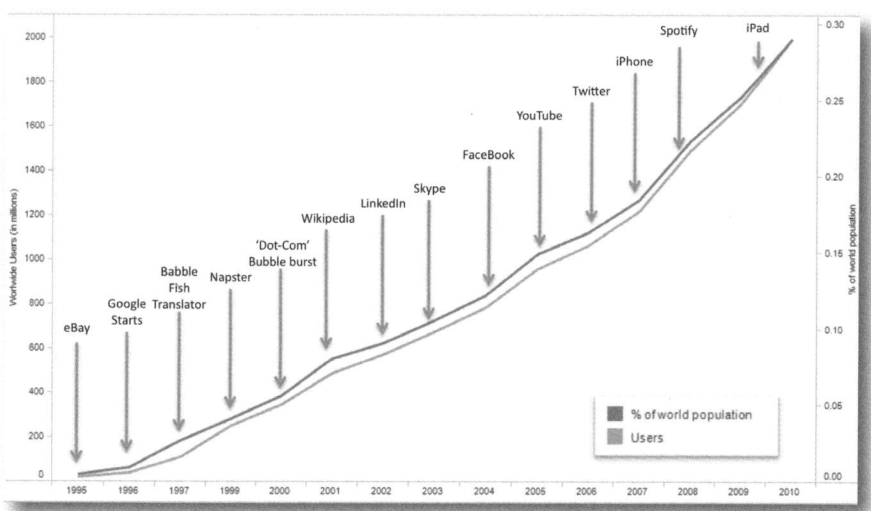

You, Your Family and the Internet 27

Chapter 3

Computer Science at university—and it was then a very new field. I have been using it in one form or another since then.

The transition from paper and telephone to instant online communications, emails, web searches, and social networks has been almost imperceptible—a gradual though rapid transition. It is worth remembering that the leading web browser—Microsoft's Internet Explorer—was first introduced as recently as August 1995. Yet, as we saw in the last chapter, that change is likely to be as significant as the network of roads built by the Romans, the printing press, the advent of radio, television, the car or air travel. Most importantly, there is simply no going back. The genie is out of the bottle, and there is no putting it back in again. Shortly after I first moved to the United States in the early 1990s, I gained a ham radio license and set up a large antenna on the roof of our house so that I could talk to my father in England without having to make expensive phone calls. Just a few years later, such endeavors are almost laughable. How easily we have become accustomed to being able to talk to friends half way around the world on Skype, or to sharing photos and news on Facebook! We expect to be able to buy almost anything online. If we need to find the nearest Chinese restaurant, we can now simply speak to our Smartphone which will "understand" what we are saying, find our current location using the built in GPS, then provide us with a list of the nearest restaurants. With the Internet we can easily retrieve information on almost any subject, or even take a look at a satellite picture of our house. Looking back, it is staggering to see how much has changed in the last ten to fifteen years. Our society and lives have changed along with it, and we have barely noticed it changing.

A fascinating site from the BBC shows how the world has increasingly adopted the Internet and laid down the infrastructure to support it.[12] In 1998 only five countries had more than 25% of the population online—the USA, Australia, New Zealand, Sweden and Iceland. By 2009, this number had increased dramatically so that almost every country in the world, with the exception of the African continent, had more than 25% of its population online while at the same time underwater cables to carry Internet traffic now crisscrossed the Atlantic and Pacific oceans. Another website[13] entitled "the evolution of the web" interactively details key Internet technologies against a timeline that starts in 1994.

Biblical Principle
Much has been written about how the Internet affects families. I was recently asked by a church in the USA to write a letter to parents on how they could effectively deal with social media. Many parents, I was told, were simply ignoring the dangers because they could not understand how the Internet worked. But being effective parents has little to do with understanding technology. The Bible speaks of bringing up our children "in the training and admonition of the Lord" (Ephesians 6:4). But how can we do this if we do not communicate and spend time with them? We must avoid the danger of only laying down rules and exasperating our children (see Ephesians 6:4, NIV) but must nurture an environment in which we lead by example, and discuss things in an open and nonthreatening environment.

Some Practical Advice
As we will see in later chapters, the Internet can not only be addictive, in the same way as other activities, but a particular danger is that it could lead to a splintering of the family unit, particularly where there are multiple computers in a household. Each member of the family spends time individually with his or her "online friends", chatting, emailing, or posting on a social network.

To counter this, why not try setting aside one evening a week as a "family night" where all members of the family engage in an activity together. Activities may, for example, include playing a game, taking a walk, or many of the myriad of other things that families can do together. Attendance, however, is mandatory.

For Discussion
Please read 2 Peter 1:5–8 and James 1:12–15. The environment in which we find ourselves is dramatically different from just a few years ago. While there is no mention of the Internet in the Bible, are there principles in these passages that can guide us?

Chapter 3

Please read Proverbs 22:6, Deuteronomy 6:7 and Colossians 3:21. What is our role as parents in protecting our families from the dangers of the Internet?

Notes

1. www.publications.parliament.uk/pa/cm200708/cmhansrd/cm080327/wmstext/80327m0001.htm
2. news.bbc.co.uk/1/hi/technology/7316700.stm
3. internet-filter-review.toptenreviews.com/internet-pornography-statistics.html#anchor5
4. *The Sun* Newspaper, dated 2 April 2009—see www.thesun.co.uk/sol/homepage/features/article2355510.ece
5. www.christianitytoday.com/ct/2008/march/20.7.html
6. *Time Magazine*, July 20, 2009
7. technology.timesonline.co.uk/tol/news/tech_and_web/article6738532.ece
8. The comment was made By Mark Driscoll in Nov 2008 at the New Frontiers conference in Brighton.
9. "Web Communities Help Patients With Rare Diseases", by Nancy Shute, National Public Radio, April 4, 2011
10. See www.sfgate.com/cgi-bin/article.cgi?f=/n/a/2009/08/30/financial/f102244D87.DTL
11. Data for this graph from www.internetworldstats.com/emarketing.htm as well as a number of sites detailing Internet history.
12. www.bbc.co.uk/news/technology-11864350
13. evolutionofweb.appspot.com/

Chapter 4

Communication

In Chapter 3, we saw the positive and negative sides of the Internet. Now we begin looking in detail at some of the key technologies that have been fueled by the Internet revolution. In particular, we consider the issue of communication. This is an area that is fraught with real and deeply troubling dangers but, when used wisely, can bring about immense benefits to individuals and organizations.

Driving While Intexticated ...

In 2007, Brandi Terry, a seventeen-year-old schoolgirl living in Utah, was on her way to visit her grandfather when she drove through a red light and crashed. In a radio interview[1] she recalls what happened: "I woke up to a bright light—I could barely open my eyes—and paramedics. This man was saying 'Brandi, Brandi,' and I just started crying. I didn't know what had happened." Terry had shattered her right ankle and broken her upper right arm in half. She couldn't walk for six months. When police checked her phone they discovered that she had sent a text within seconds of the accident. Even after recovery, she went on to say of her habit of texting while driving: "I tried really, really hard not to. Then it got to the point where I would do it only once every 5 minutes," she says. "I don't know—it's just so addicting, I just can't put it down." So why did she do it?

Email Addiction

In a March 2008 BBC report, Professor Cary Cooper, who advises the British government on stress in the workplace, suggested that "email is one of the most pernicious stressors of our time."[2] He went on to say that every year Britons take 14 million sick days due to stress and that email is a major source of employee anxiety. "We are 24/7, we are interfaced by the mobile phone, by Blackberry, by emails, by a whole range of technologies, so that we are almost on call all the time." This phenomenon is happening all over the world.

Wherever we look, we find people addicted to checking messages on

Chapter 4

their mobile phones. How often have we seen a row of teenagers sitting together, all glued to their phones with ear buds firmly in place? Perhaps we have perversely wondered if they were in fact communicating with each other—by text!

Teenagers are not the only ones guilty of such behavior as anyone who has been on a flight can testify. As soon as the plane lands, out come the Smartphones to check up on that message that might just have been missed.

Or take the case of a man being interviewed for a head-teacher's position. He was unable to stop himself checking his phone in the middle of the interview, as soon as he received a text message. He did not get the job.

Emails Can Get You Fired …

Much care should always be taken when sending emails. Not only are they admissible as evidence in court but they can easily be misinterpreted.

A chief executive of an American health care company, Cerner Corporation, wrote an email that turned out to be disastrous for the company as well as the morale of company employees. In the email, employees were accused of being lazy and managers were also threatened with being fired. It seemed the employee parking lot was not full at 8am and was nearly empty by 5pm each day. After the email showed up on a Yahoo Financial Message Board, investors began questioning the leadership of the company. The result was a plunge of 22% in the share price of the company's stock on Wall Street.

Or consider the case of Vicki Walker, an accountant from Auckland, New Zealand, who was fired for sending emails to work colleagues that "caused disharmony in the workplace". The company she worked for, ProCare Health, claimed that her emails advising colleagues how to complete staff claim forms were confrontational because of the use of a sentence written all in capital letters and highlighted in blue with the time and date highlighted in red. For these "crimes against humanity", Walker was fired from the position she had held at the company for two years.

It's All About Me

So why do we do it? Why are so many addicted to new media? The Webster's Dictionary defines addiction in these words: "To surrender oneself to something obsessively or habitually." This seems to be a very apt description of what is going on.

It seems to be an innate part of our psyche, a need to feel wanted, or perhaps just our selfish human nature that makes us want to think that we are indispensable; so much so, that we become addicted to email, text, twitter, Facebook or any number of new communications media. We need people to know that we are here and somehow to feel that someone "cares" about our world. Increasingly, people are finding it hard to give up being interconnected with others all of the time.

This was brought up by some research at the University of Maryland, reported in their "World Unplugged" survey.[3] The study asked nearly a thousand students in ten countries on five continents—from Chile to China, Lebanon to the USA, Uganda to the United Kingdom—to abstain from using all media for a full day. According to the study, four in five students reported symptoms of distress, confusion and isolation within a mere twenty-four hours of logging off. A clear majority even failed to complete the voluntary twenty-four hour period.

Professor Susan Moeller, research leader, said, "Students talked about how scary it was, how addicted they were. They expected the frustration. But they didn't expect to have the psychological effects, to be lonely, to be panicked, the anxiety, literally heart palpitations."

Participants in the study are quoted as saying, "Media is not just a convenience; it is literally a part of my life," and, "I can't be without knowing what people are saying and feeling, where they are, and what's happening."

Do You Tweet?

Another new technology that has people baffled is Twitter. Started in 2006, it has experienced a monthly growth of 1,382%. Twitter is a service that makes it possible for people to send and receive messages of up to 140 characters, known as "tweets". Anyone can subscribe to receive tweets from friends or celebrities. Some of the biggest showbiz stars and politicians have massive followings. Three-and-a-half million people follow every tweet that Britney Spears sends, while two-and-a-half million need to know about Barack Obama's every move.

Twitter (as well as Facebook) has had a significant political impact at the beginning of the second decade of the twenty-first century. The *Boston Globe* reported that "the sites served as a means of communication that helped spur reform movements in Tunisia, Egypt, Libya, and elsewhere in the Arab world—accomplishing goals that had eluded US policymakers for years."[4] It was Twitter, for example, that was at the heart of the protests in Iran because it was both very easy for the average citizen to use and very hard for any central authority to control.

New Media Benefits
There is much that can be said in favor of new media. Text messages and mobile phones can be of great value in times of emergency. Or consider the charitable organization that has been able to cut costs significantly by replacing letters with emails. Instantly, such groups can let people know of needs, of a difficult situation, or a matter for rejoicing. Organizations such as The Christian Institute in the UK and others are even using Twitter to keep subscribers informed of significant developments. Mike Judge, from the Christian Institute, explains: "Over 10,000 individuals are signed up to receive email alerts from The Christian Institute. It is a quick, cheap and versatile way of informing people about important issues. To send out the same information by post would take days to prepare and would cost thousands. We simply wouldn't have the resources to do it."

Or think of parents, separated from their married children and grandchildren, who can now see them and talk to them using free Internet video services such as Skype. These days the world is a much smaller place.

All this is changing the way that we interact with each other while at the same time undoubtedly contributing to a higher level of stress. People are expected to be available all the time. The boss gives employees a Blackberry and expects to be able to call on their services any time of night and day.

Communication

Tracking friends with Google Latitude[5]

But the change is here to stay, as the postal service will attest, with a 10% yearly drop in the physical mail that we send. There is no going back. We live in a world where we are available all of the time. There are even iPhone and Android Apps to track our movements via a GPS cell phone and which let us know which of our friends are nearby.

Biblical Principles
When considering our 24/7 society, we need to remind ourselves of the key principles of self-control, selflessness and service. In the Bible, the Book of James explains it most clearly when it states that "where envy and self-seeking exist, confusion and every evil thing *are* there. But the wisdom that is from above is first pure, then peaceable, gentle, willing to yield, full of mercy and good fruits, without partiality and without hypocrisy." (James 3:16–17, italics mine).

In contrast to what is going on around us, we are to take care not to be

Chapter 4

addicted to email, text, Twitter or any new form of communications. These are tools to be used for good. They are not to control us.

We should also apply the principles found later in the same Bible book and "be swift to hear, slow to speak, slow to wrath" (James 1:19). In other words, we need to think about how we communicate with people. We need, for example, to consider how a person might read or misinterpret an email. Our response should be considered, measured and focused on building up others.

Practical Advice

With spam accounting for over 90% of all email traffic, it is important to take simple steps, such as installing a spam filter (though many email providers such as Google and BT already have these), and using up-to-date antivirus software. However, beyond these things, basic principles such as self-control or thoughtfulness are critically important.

Some couples have found that sharing an email account can be helpful. Others suggest that not responding to emails or text messages immediately is a good way of avoiding their addictive effects. Particularly helpful is the idea of not responding to a message on the same day it was received if it has upset us. Simply putting it in the "drafts" folder and re-reading it the following day before sending it can avoid many dangers.

Let me conclude with this true story that can be applied to all forms of new communications. Two friends were together outside chopping up logs. The phone in the house rang several times, and eventually one friend asked the other if he was going to answer it. The homeowner simply said, "No. The phone is a convenience, and, at this moment, it is not convenient."

For Discussion

Please read James 1:16–20, 2 Peter 1:5–8, and Philippians 2:1–4. What do these passages tell us about how we are to deal with most communications today that seem to focus on immediacy and our motivations for being available all of the time?

Please read Matthew 6:5–6, Mark 1:35 and Genesis 24:63. Is it necessary for us to be always available? If not, why not?

Notes

1 www.npr.org/templates/story/story.php?storyId=113132868
2 news.bbc.co.uk/1/hi/business/7281707.stm
3 See theworldunplugged.wordpress.com/about/statistics/, also www.thedrum.co.uk/news/2011/04/08/20499-study-finds-tech-addicts-mimic-drug-addicts-in-withdrawal/
4 "In the Middle East, the US should learn from Facebook's success" by **Alan Wirzbicki** The *Boston Globe*, April 8, 2011
5 Image taken from Google latitude website

Chapter 5

Facebook and the Social Network Revolution

In February 2009, the *Daily Telegraph*[1] reported that Kimberly Swann, a sixteen-year-old from Clacton, England, posted on Facebook that she thought her job was boring. She was called into her manager's office and handed a letter that cited her Facebook comments as the reason for dismissal:

"Following your comments made on Facebook about your job and the company we feel it is better that, as you are not happy and do not enjoy your work, we end your employment with immediate effect."

Unbecoming Behavior

Stacy Snyder wanted to be a teacher. By the spring of 2006, the twenty-five-year-old single mother had completed her course and was looking forward to her future career. Then her dream died. Summoned by university officials, she was told she would not be a teacher, because she had posted a photo on the Internet showing her in costume wearing a pirate's hat and drinking from a plastic cup. This was deemed to be behavior unbecoming of a teacher.[2] Stacy considered taking the photo offline. But the damage was done. Her web page had been catalogued by search engines, and her photo archived by web crawlers. The Internet remembered what Stacy wanted to have forgotten.

Presidential Warning

Even President Obama, in a September 2009 televised address to American schools, advised them to "be careful what you post on Facebook. Whatever you do, it will be pulled up later in your life."[3]

Nonetheless social networks have emerged as the most popular web phenomena. One reason for this is that social networks can be useful for making contact with people you may have lost touch with, such as school

Facebook and the Social Network Revolution

or university friends. It helps keep family and friends abreast of what each is doing, without having to write, email or make phone contact.

There are many social networks including MySpace, and specialist networks such as LinkedIn for business users, GovLoop for US government employees, or Groupons to let you know of special offers available in your area. However, the best known and most successful is, without doubt, Facebook.

Person of the Year

When Mark Zuckerberg was named person of the year for 2010 by *Time Magazine*, it reflected the impact that Facebook is having on our society. As a nineteen-year-old sophomore at Harvard University, Zuckerberg started a web service that was billed as "an online directory that connects people through social networks at colleges". The idea was to reflect the kinds of interactions that students may have with one another. In early 2011, Facebook added its 550 millionth member and is currently growing at a rate of about 700,000 people a day. In other words, roughly one out of every ten people on the planet has a Facebook account and, by the end of 2010, the site accounted for one out of four American page views.

The 2009 Oxford Dictionary "Word of the Year"

For most people who started talking to others on the Internet using Instant Messaging (IM), social networks provide a much richer set of capabilities. Not only can you chat to your friends online, you can also see messages they post about what they are doing, pictures, events, birthdays, or even play games together. A network is made up of people who have applied to join with you and become your friend. It is possible to set up a network so that only friends can view your pictures or see what you write on your wall. Should you choose, you can remove people from your social network at any time. To remove someone is to "unfriend" them, a word that was adopted as the new 2009 "Word of the Year" by the Oxford Dictionary.

Some of the Dangers of Facebook

So why worry about it? While many have accounts on Facebook, it is

Chapter 5

particularly teenagers that seem to be the most active. Should we be concerned about whether our teenagers are on the site or not, or how much time they spend on it? Is this not something that teenagers do, and that will go away as they grow up? Teenagers have always met together as groups and interacted about every imaginable aspect of their lives. They have always met people at school, college or elsewhere that parents have had no idea about. They have shared pictures, music and talked about all sorts of issues. Whether they use physical pictures, text, phone or now Facebook, are they not simply doing what teenagers have always done?

These, in my view, are fair questions to ask. In one sense, I would agree that teenagers are no different now than they have ever been. However, while there are real benefits to Facebook, there are also real dangers. Let me suggest a few.

IT'S PERMANENT

What is posted on Facebook can been seen by others, and may be there for a very long time. Perhaps many of us can remember doing things as teenagers that would now embarrass us. The difference, however, is that the consequences of these things are almost certainly long gone. The same cannot be said of Facebook, whose records may linger far longer than we might imagine. Employers, college admission tutors and others now regularly check Facebook. What happens when they come across that picture, or that comment, that was posted in a moment of folly?

WHAT IS A "FRIEND"?

Another issue comes with the rather loose definition of "friend" in most social networks. Perhaps, like me, you have accepted an invitation from someone you met a few times to become your "friend". After the initial brief encounter, you have not seen that person again, but have been kept informed of events in his or her life through Facebook, even "liking" such comments from time to time. Then comes the unforeseen event of meeting this "friend" again in real life. You find that, in fact, you have very little to say, know little about that person in reality, and the conversation soon dries up.

Facebook and the Social Network Revolution

One of the reviewers of this book points out how "friending" someone can lead to unforeseen consequences:

A girl from our church sadly went "off the rails", posting all kinds of lurid details about her life that she might one day regret. Because many of the young people in the church were her Facebook friends, they ended up reading these and wondered why the church wasn't doing anything about it. The church elders, of course, didn't know the extent of the problem, because, on principle, we were not "friends" with any of the girls.4

IT COMES INTO YOUR HOME
We generally make a point of finding out a little about people we invite into our homes, especially if they accompany our children. However, with Facebook, we invite people into our home, and onto our children's computer, Smartphone or other device. We are allowing them in, and giving them the capability to share information about our everyday lives as well as our family life, since at any moment information may well be posted about what is happening in the family circle.

IT CAN BECOME AN OBSESSION
Facebook can easily become addictive. That is the genius of the site. Why it is addictive is another matter, and one that psychologists can argue about. But most of us somehow feel compelled to share. The younger generation, in particular, is known to be open and share details of everything. They want to know what's going on with friends and need to think that others care about what they are doing and thinking. As with texting, there seems to be a need to check Facebook several times a day (and, in some cases, several times in an hour!). Some of the games on Facebook are equally addictive. Witness the meteoric rise of games such as Farmville or Mafia Wars.

IDENTITY THEFT
Teenagers are particularly prone to be uncaring about self-disclosure and the kind and quantity of information they share. In a 2009 study,5 researchers developed a tool to score the information disclosed on

Chapter 5

Facebook. What they found was that as age increases, less personal information is disclosed. In other words, older people are more cautious when disclosing personal information. We should be concerned that teenagers are getting roped into revealing most of their identities. The most common and important danger is identity theft; many fake profiles have been created based on live information from real people's profiles.

ENTRAPMENT

The following news report of a trial that took place in Manchester, England, helps us to understand the dangers:

> A pedophile terrorized a schoolgirl on the social networking website Facebook after duping her into accepting him as a "friend". Robert Sumner stalked the teenager online and bombarded her with texts demanding she meet him. When she refused he told her he knew where she lived—and threatened to rape her … Judge Iain Hamilton said the girl's mother had "wrongly" allowed her daughter access to the social networking site and said the case highlighted the dangers of youngsters using them.[6]

CREATING A FALSE EXISTENCE

Even the Pope is aware of this. In 2011 he called it "Enclosing oneself in a sort of parallel existence, or excessive exposure to the virtual world."[7] One commentator explains that

> at university, I knew students who spent hours cultivating their Facebook pages every day. They had to look popular and busy on the website, because on some level they thought it would translate into real life. But strangely, it was always those with hundreds of Facebook 'friends'—or thousands of Twitter followers—who seemed to be the most lonely … A 'parallel existence' online means sitting, on planet earth, in front of a computer screen[8].

What is Facebook All About?

One of the things that we need to realize is that Facebook is not an altruistic, innocent venture. It's all about money. Even if its creator Mark Zuckerberg is said to be indifferent about his fortune, Facebook backers are not, and the fact that it is worth billions of dollars is important to them.

Facebook and the Social Network Revolution

How does Facebook make its money? Through advertising. This is its genius. Advertising on television may be somewhat indiscriminate in its focus. Online advertising with Google is somewhat more targeted, as it requires someone to click on a link, with the assumption that the pundit is interested in what he or she has clicked on. With Facebook, however, advertisers can specifically target by interest, gender, age and a host of other things, often based on what friends like or do not like. We live in a world where one in ten people is connected through a single social network, and advertisers love this. The holy grail of advertising is getting friends to recommend products to other friends. This is exactly what Facebook can provide. Making money is not necessarily a bad thing, but we need to be aware of what motivates sites like Facebook.

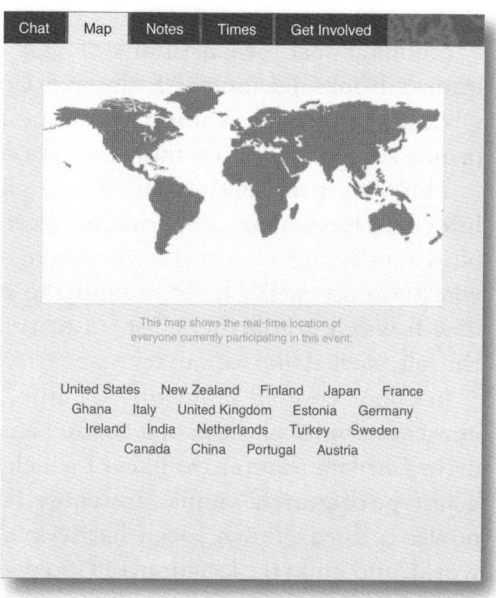

An image from the LiveChurch.tv website showing online 'worshipers' at a Sunday service (used with permission).

All You Need is Online

Other problems come to the fore when looking at a special kind of social network, such as the "online church". This kind of church is not simply a web site, and neither is it a way of downloading sermons (whether audio or video) or even simply live steaming of a church message. It is far more than this, and is intended to replace conventional churches with online equivalents. The online church websites provide social networks or link into Facebook so that those listening or viewing on their computers can "chat to one another" during the service, share thoughts or ideas, or receive support from a pastoral assistant at any time.

Chapter 5

In a blog post for ChristianityToday.com,[9] Bob Hyatt, a pastor who leads a brick-and-mortar Evergreen Community Church in Portland, Oregon, writes that calling an online church a virtual church "gives people the idea that everything they need is available here."

This is precisely what Craig Groeschel, senior pastor at LifeChurch.tv—an online church—said in a CNN interview, "We were blown away at how people could actually worship along [online]. The whole family will gather around the computer, and they'll sing and they'll worship together. Instead of trying to get people to come to a church, we feel like we can take a church to them."[10]

In a book entitled *SimChurch*[11] author Douglas Estes says that "today a new community of the people of God has begun ... A change is occurring in the Christian church the likes of which has not happened in centuries ... This type of church is unlike any church the world has ever seen. It has the power to break down social barriers, unite believers from all over the world, and build the kingdom of God with a widow's mite of financing. It is a completely different type of church from any the world has ever seen."

We can imagine the benefits of such an arrangement for some—for example, the Christian in an Islamic country, or a missionary isolated from any other believers. However, there are significant dangers for those who could otherwise attend a good church. As with other social media, relationships are not real, but based on the comments and persona that each online user projects. How can a pastor "shepherd the flock of God" (1 Peter 5:2) or help people in a crisis if he effectively knows nothing about them and could never meet with them? Or how can such a church reach out to the local community?

Are There Any Benefits?

There are indeed benefits. To some, perhaps most, it is simply an innocent and relaxing pastime, connecting with friends and family, some of which may live in another country altogether. In an article in the *Journal of Adolescent Research*, one researcher concluded that "benefits of online interaction for teens outweighed the dangers."[12] The article goes on to say that "in online discussions, teenagers have the opportunity to develop critical thinking and argumentation skills. They can find support from online peer groups, explore questions of identity, get help with homework, and ask questions about sensitive issues they might be afraid to ask face to face. They can develop their skills in understanding issues from the perspective of others."

For the Christian church family, it can provide the opportunity to stay in touch with missionaries, for example, who might otherwise feel very isolated. For others, it can help provide real insight into the emotional state of a friend in order to provide support and help.

Biblical Principles

There are several biblical principles that should be considered when thinking about our use of social networks. These include the principle of self-control (one aspect of the fruit of the Spirit—Galatians 5:23) as well as taking care of how we live—something we touched on in the previous chapter: "So then, my beloved brethren, let every man be swift to hear, slow to speak, slow to wrath" (James 1:19). Other principles include avoiding addiction, something we will explore further later in this book.

However, one of the key principles is the importance of being transparent and not pretending to be something other than what we are. The Bible puts it this way: "Above all, my brethren, do not swear, either by heaven or by earth or with any other oath. But let your 'Yes' be 'Yes,' and your 'No,' 'No,' lest you fall into judgment." (James 5:12). In other words, there should be no pretense about us. The term we use to describe someone who pretends to be something other than he or she is, is hypocrite, a term derived from the ancient Greek actors who would wear a mask (*hypokrisis*) during a performance. The Bible has much to say about hypocrisy. In the New Testament, hypocrisy was attributed to the Pharisee sect and repeatedly condemned by the Lord Jesus Christ (Matthew 5:8, Luke 13:15). King Solomon even wrote a proverb about it:

The hypocrite with his mouth destroys his neighbor,
But through knowledge the righteous will be delivered.   (Proverbs 11:9)

Practical Advice

While the use of social networks affects both adults and children, it is a

Chapter 5

particular worry to parents wondering what they should do about Facebook. This is a decision that needs to be made individually and as a matter of conscience. Some parents have decided that Facebook should not be part of their family life. Others have limited time on the site (as far as they can tell), and some have an open policy. Whatever decision is made, however, it must be made after carefully considering the potential dangers and benefits, all weighed up in the light of our understanding of our own children. What we must avoid is a tendency either to completely ignore or exonerate Facebook of any potential danger, or to blame Facebook for all our woes. Sin is from within, though we must also be wise to avoid exposing our children to harm. For some, banning Facebook will work, but for many, it will not, as children will probably find a way to create and maintain a Facebook presence anyway.

Some commonsense advice may help. We should:

- Discuss the measure of personal information being revealed. We should check security settings on Facebook, and make sure that any information is only shared with friends.
- All of us, no matter how young or old, should be wary of revealing information such as age, gender, location, height, weight, measurements, address, and school/college location for online strangers to see.
- We should stop and think before posting any information online, especially when posting photos. These could be embarrassing in the future and negatively affect situations such as educational or job prospects. The rule should always be this: if in doubt, don't post it.
- We should look for constructive ways of using Facebook, such as getting in touch with missionaries. In fact, this could be a regular family activity!
- When dealing with our children, we need to also be consistent. It's no good getting annoyed with our teenagers for spending too much time on Facebook if we are equally obsessed by anything else—be it television, sport, or a myriad of other distractions. For example, some have adopted a "phones on the fridge" while at home for every member of the family. This may stop our teenagers texting too much, but would be hypocritical if we were unable to avoid the

temptation to check our Smartphone for that important email we have been waiting for. Let's be consistent!

Above all, let's be involved. Teenagers, in particular, by their very nature want to push against the boundaries, explore everything, and they lack self-control. But they also want to know that there are boundaries. Raising children is a hugely difficult undertaking. But in a church family there are usually others who have been through what we are experiencing. We should not be afraid to ask for their advice and prayerful support.

For Discussion

Please read Titus 2:1–8, Romans 12:9–13 and Ephesians 4:24. Are there practical steps that you can take in your local church to help support each other to avoid the dangers of social networks while also taking advantage of what they have to offer?

Please read Ephesians 6:21–22, Proverbs 11:13, 14:23 and Matthew 5:37. Is it right to share information with other "friends", some of whom we barely know? What are the dangers?

Notes

1 www.telegraph.co.uk/technology/facebook/4838076/Office-worker-sacked-for-branding-work-boring-on-Facebook.html
2 **Viktor Mayer-Schönberger,** *Delete: The Virtue of Forgetting in The Digital Age* (Princeton University Press, 2009), p1
3 Quoted in the *Washington Times*, Sep 8, 2009.
4 Cited by the pastor of a church in the UK
5 Reported in www.shockmd.com/2010/01/04/the-dangers-of-facebook/
6 UK *Daily Mail*, Oct 26, 2010
7 From catholicHerald.co.uk 13 Feb 2011
8 Ibid
9 see bobhyatt.typepad.com/
10 See www.cnn.com/2009/TECH/11/13/online.church.services/index.html
11 **Douglas C. Estes,** *Simchurch: Being the Church in the Virtual World* (Zondervan 2009). From Chapter 1 of the e-Book.
12 ScienceDaily, Nov. 8, 2007

Chapter 6

Pornography

In the first part of this book, we have considered aspects of the Internet that can have both positive and negative ramifications. Sadly, there is no escaping the subject that we now need to consider. There are no positive benefits, only sinful, dark, negative and life-destroying consequences. No one who has an email account or browsed the Internet for more than a few minutes can have escaped the intrusive dark shadow cast by this wicked and money-driven industry.

Pornography Ruins Lives

Let's make no mistake about it, pornography is all about money. The online pornography industry generates some $10B per year.[1] It is a vicious and deeply addictive industry, taking advantage of base human desires, preying on the weak, and destroying lives. The heart-wrenching testimony of "J", a twenty-six-year-old man addicted to Internet pornography, illustrates this:

> I go to work, I go to school, and I spend time with my family. The people around me don't know that I'm a shell of a person. They don't have a clue that I don't feel my life is worth living ... I grew more and more consumed by looking at pornography on the Internet for hours on end ... I grew more and more angry at the world ... There's no way to undo it now. The only thing that numbs the pain digs me that much deeper into the hole ... I have ruined my life, and I did it one day at a time as I sat down in front of my computer yet again.[2]

Responding to "J", Max says:

> What a sad story. I can feel his pain right now. I was a porn addict myself. I know how destructive this thing is. It doesn't let you think of anything, it breaks you slowly

Pornography

mentally and physically. Porn addicts find no interest in anything, they don't even like to be social, the world becomes a hell for them. This feeling takes them to depression—you stop believing in yourself, you feel like a criminal all of the time. In short it just destroys your life.[3]

Statistics
Pornography is easily found on the Internet. Here are a few statistics:
- There are 4.2 million websites (12% of total websites).
- Every day, 1 in 4 search requests (68 million) and 2.5 billion emails (8% of total emails or 4.5 for every Internet user) are about pornography.[4]
- The average age of first exposure to Internet porn is 11.[5]
- 90% of 8–16 year olds have viewed porn online mostly while doing homework[6].

This problem is not restricted to men. One in six women (17%), including Christians, struggles with pornography addiction.[7]

Don't Try a Second Life
Just a few years ago, the buzz in the Internet world and in the media was all about Second Life. People would immerse themselves for hours at a time, in this virtual world, first creating computer representations of themselves (avatars) and then flying around a computer world populated by other people's avatars, buildings and events. Anxious not to be left out of a potential lucrative market, some large corporations set up virtual stores. General Motors, for example, set up what US television news channel CNN called a "make-believe dealership"[8] to promote their cars. Today, most of Second Life is deserted, except for one virtual "island". In 2007, after some high-profile investigations by the FBI in the US over online gambling activities, Second Life owners decided to try to clean up their act. They closed down all virtual casinos (where real money was being gambled) and relocated its "adult" content to a separate virtual continent called Zindra. Today, the vast majority of the activity of Second Life can be found on Zindra, a place which, according to one reporter, is full of "downright disturbing activities taking place".[9]

Chapter 6

A deeply troubling French movie, *Black Heaven*, featured in the 2010 Cannes Festival, bears an uncanny resemblance to Second Life. It provides some insights into the blurring of reality with an imaginary world, with overtones of suicide pacts and sexual activity.

Second Life is not a place for Christians and serves to vividly illustrate how things have a natural propensity to degenerate to evil.

Churches Are Not Immune

In a fascinating article, John Steley, a British Christian psychologist who has lectured at the London Theological Seminary on Internet abuse, writes:

> I work with people from a large number of Christian churches and mission societies, including some of the most conservative and evangelical. What I am told by those I meet leads me to conclude that the use of Internet pornography is a significant problem in the church today. None of us should consider ourselves to be immune from this temptation.[10]

Other surveys have confirmed this. A recent US based scholarly report concluded that "subscriptions [to pornographic websites] are more prevalent in US States where surveys indicate conservative positions on religion, gender roles, and sexuality."[11] Ironically, the report goes to say that "in such regions, a statistically significant smaller proportion of subscriptions begin on Sundays, compared with other regions".

Even pastors are not immune. An organization dedicated to helping Christians who struggle with Internet pornography explains that 53% of Christian men consume pornography, 51% of pastors say porn is a temptation, while 37% of pastors say that it is currently a struggle and 18% of pastors look at porn a couple of times a month.[12] Other studies confirm the problem. An Internet survey conducted by Rick Warren of Saddleback Church found that 30% of 6,000 pastors had viewed Internet porn in the last 30 days.[13]

It is simply not good enough to bury our heads in the sand and pretend that Internet pornography happens "somewhere else". We cannot hide behind the pretense that it cannot affect us or our church. The privacy that the Internet affords provides the opportunity to visit pornographic websites without anyone else knowing about it. How many church members, pastors, young people, deacons, elders, youth workers hide a secret addiction? Can we really say that we are immune?

World Magazine, a US Christian weekly publication, reported about a "Mr. Burgin" who, for twenty years was a churchgoer and preacher and was "trusted, revered, and believed to be of impeccable reputation". But beneath the thick varnish of smooth oration and doctrinally sound sermons, this conservative pastor secretly harbored a monster. "I was a master of duplicity," Mr. Burgin said of his addiction to Internet pornography. For the entirety of his ministry and even before, Mr. Burgin tumbled silently through a cycle of shame, repentance, and broken vows... Despite a guilt-ridden conscience, Mr. Burgin often preached on sexual purity, slogging through such sermons undetected. "I compartmentalized it in my mind," he said. "I rationalized. I minimized." When discovered, his ministry and family lost, his reputation soiled, Mr. Burgin turned to the church for help and found little. "Churches didn't know how to handle me," he said.[14]

An article in *Christianity Today* sheds further light, "Don't assume that porn isn't a problem in the church. One evangelical leader was skeptical of survey findings that said 50 percent of Christian men have looked at porn recently. So he surveyed his own congregation. He found that 60 percent had done so within the past year, and 25 percent within the past 30 days. Other surveys reveal that one in three visitors to adult websites are women."[15]

Some Key Principles

There can be no doubt that pornography in any form, whether Internet-based or not, is wrong. In seeking to deal with this issue, we should consider the following principles:

Self-examination

This is perhaps not often emphasized for the fear of introspection or of the modern obsession with self. Yet, even in the Bible, we are called to examine ourselves (see 1 Corinthians 11:28, Galatians 6:4). If we have a particular weakness, we are told to "flee" from it (1 Corinthians 6:18, 1 Timothy 6:11). The Bible confirms that we all have individual weaknesses when it speaks of being drawn away by our own "desires and enticed" (James 1:14–15). If this sin of sexual immorality or pornography is one that is a particular weakness for some, they must first recognize this, and then both seek help, and stay well clear of anything (especially on the Internet) that could lead to this particular sin.[16]

This particular issue is even in evidence in the Bible, with examples that include King David, who was unable to stop himself from lusting after a woman and then committing adultery with her (2 Samuel 11). The problem of sexual immorality can affect even the best of people. Self-examination and self-control are two sides of the same coin: know who you are, and take care to control your weaknesses.

Accountability

We live in an age where we are told that "whatever people do in the privacy of their own home" is their business. In the minds of some, Internet pornography is justified because it "does no harm" to anyone and is something that is done in the privacy of a home. Yet, as we have already seen, this is simply not true. It eats away at people's lives and leaves them empty and devastated. It breaks up marriages and tears down families. One day, we will also have to give an account to a Holy God for all our thoughts, words, actions and inactions (Matthew 12:36, Romans 14:12). In addition, the Bible emphasizes the idea of mutual accountability (Hebrews 13:17, James 5:16). This is a very important and somewhat forgotten principle. In a church we are part of a family of believers and, because of this, we need to learn to depend on one another—receiving advice and support, as well as giving it (1 Corinthians 12). We are to develop a familial openness with one another, a desire to share, to help, and, most difficult of all, a willingness to be helped. The strength of mutual accountability is an area that even the secular organization *Alcoholics Anonymous* has recognized with its "buddy system" and a practice that could be said to be responsible for much of its success.

Pornography

Practical Advice

FIND A "BUDDY"

John Steley, the Christian psychologist mentioned earlier in this chapter, has worked in this area (johnsteley.co.uk). He provides the following advice:

- Tell a trusted person about the problem. This may be your pastor, home-group leader, or another mature Christian. Ask this person to enquire regularly about your Internet use.
- Use an Internet accountability program. You will be asked to name a number of people who will receive regular emails telling them what sites you have accessed. Examples of these include *Covenant Eyes* (www.covenanteyes.com) which is already used by a number of churches.
- Think carefully about the people you name for your accountability program. Ideally, they should be people with whom you have regular contact and whom you respect.
- Make sure you have an accountability program operating on every computer to which you have access.
- If possible place your computer somewhere that others can see the screen.
- If you feel that the urge to use pornography is irresistible, try putting it off until some time later. You may find that by then the urge has gone or is at a level you can resist.
- Ask yourself what need pornography is filling in your life. Is there a need for greater intimacy? More excitement or adventure? Do you just have too much idle time? You may find yourself thinking:
  - "Just a little bit will not do any harm."
  - "I need to know what is out there so I can inform others."
  - "Everyone does something wrong. This is just my particular failing."
  - "This is not what I find most titillating."
  - "Looking at this might help my sex life," or something similar.

These are rationalizations. You need to focus on something else. (See Philippians 4:8)

Chapter 6

- Remind yourself, people who produce pornography are only after your money.
- If you fail, do not punish yourself. Ask God's forgiveness. Maybe tell a trusted friend, and do something useful. (Try having a list of useful things to do and have them to hand.)
- If you go for even a short time without viewing pornography, tell yourself, "Well done!"
- Remember. Most addictive problems do not go away easily. You will probably need to persevere for some time—until not using Internet pornography becomes a lifestyle. Give yourself regular encouragement and tell yourself the goal is worth it.

PROTECT THE COMPUTER
In addition to John Steley's wise advice, there are a number of extra steps which we can take. One of the more worrying developments is illustrated by the story of a man who was charged with child pornography because indecent pictures were found on his computer. In fact, these had been "stored" there by a pedophile, using a virus to infect his computer so that the criminal intruder could use it to store disgusting pictures and thereby evade the risk of being found in possession of this material.[17] The best way to counter this problem is to have an antivirus program on each computer, (being sure that the antivirus program is kept up to date), and to make sure that the firewall is switched on—a firewall comes integrated into Windows and Apple Mac computers.

INSTALL A FAMILY FILTER
These are pieces of software that filter out sites with pornographic or other undesirable content. The *Covenant Eyes* software is a specialized example of this. Others include a number of commercial products such as *Net Nanny* (www.netnanny.com), *SafeEyes* (www.internetsafety.com) or *Blue Coat* (www.k9webprotection.com). There are also iPhone apps that do a similar job. Installing these will prevent accidentally wandering into some undesirable site, and also help to prevent children, in particular, from viewing pornography. There are ways around this software (particularly for the one who possesses the administrator

password), but, even then, it will help quell the initial temptation and may stop accidental exposure by children using the computer.

KEEP AWAY

For some, the answer may be to stay away from computers. Understanding our particular failings, and being honest with ourselves, is vitally important. If you or someone you know has this failing, I would urge you to pray and to seek counsel (perhaps with your pastor, elder or trusted Christian friend). Don't wait until it is too late …

For Discussion

Please read Galatians 6:1–5, 1 Corinthians 10:11–13 and James 1:14. In the "nurture versus nature" debate, are different people subject to different types of sinful tendencies? Why do you think this is important?

Please read Galatians 6:2 and Romans 14:1–13. Why is mutual accountability not spoken of more today? What are the characteristics that you might look for in someone to whom you might be willing to be accountable?

Notes

1 www.christianity.com/Christian%20Living/Features/11558259/
2 www.quitpornaddiction.com/true-stories/i-have-ruined-my-life-one-day-at-a-time-js-story/
3 Ibid.
4 www.restoringsexualpurity.org/statistics/
5 Family Safe Media, December 15, 2005
6 internet-filter-review.toptenreviews.com/internet-pornography-statistics.html
7 Today's Christian Woman, 2003, quoted in www.freedomyou.com/addiction/Internet_Pornography.htm
8 See articles.cnn.com/2006-11-17/business/2nd_life_cars_1_dealership-virtual-world-reuben-steiger?_s=PM:AUTOS
9 From the article on Second Life in the January 2010 issue of PC PRO
10 *Evangelicals Now*—October 2007
11 Red Light States: Who Buys Online Adult Entertainment? by **Benjamin Edelman,** found in the *Journal of Economic Perspectives*—Volume 23, Number 1—Winter 2009
12 xxxchurch.com/gethelp/pastors/stats.html

Chapter 6

13 Quoted in www.worldmag.com/articles/10555
14 *World Magazine*, April 23, 2005
15 *Christianity Today*, March 7, 2008
16 As hard as it may be to accept this point, it is even possible that children may inherit some of the same weakness as their parents have.
17 See "Framed for child porn—by a PC virus", by **Jordan Robertson,** AP Technology Writer—Mon Nov 9, 2009 , www.msnbc.msn.com/id/33778733

Chapter 7

If It's Free, Then You Are The Product ...

You may have heard the saying that "Google knows everything." What this generally means is that when we use the Google search engine, almost all knowledge is accessible to us on the Internet. By 2008, Google claimed[1] to have indexed over 1 trillion unique web pages (that is 1,000,000,000,000) with hundreds of thousands being added every day. In this chapter, we will also consider how companies use the Internet to market and sell products, including dubious practices such as "viral marketing" and the abuse of personal information. Not only do Google (and other search engines) know a great deal about the Internet, it may be surprising to learn how much Internet marketing companies know about us.

Identity Theft

The Internet has opened up a vast amount of knowledge, including information about individuals. This is something that can be sold. Some of this activity is illegal; much of it is perfectly within the confines of the law.

One senior fraud expert explained that criminals are exploiting the same data-mining techniques that are used by banks and governments to spot fraud. To put this in context, a senior British Telecom executive explained that "for a small fee, $50 (£30) or thereabouts, [these companies will] gather all the data on you and prepare a three- to five-page detailed report. The fee implies this exercise probably took less than an hour."[2] Let's put this in context, however. With billions of people using the Internet, it is very unlikely that someone is watching everything that you type. The data used in identity fraud is usually gathered automatically. A favorite approach is to trick an Internet user into downloading a program called a "key logger". This small piece of software installs itself on a user's system, then tracks what is being typed

Chapter 7

on the keyboard. It then automatically uploads information of interest to a server, such as username and passwords to various sites. It is this information that is being "harvested" automatically, then sold to third parties. In recent years, you may have noticed that banks and financial organizations have asked you to use a keypad and enter a randomly assigned pin, or to select from a screen pictures that are displayed in a different location every time you sign in. These are techniques that have been developed to reduce the impact of key loggers. Most antivirus software will also detect these programs.

If It's Free, Then You Are The Product

Everyone likes something free. Google is free, as is Facebook and hundreds of thousands of other websites. But as the saying goes, if it's free, what they are selling is information about you—you are the product.

Over the last few years, or in other words since most people began using the Internet, we have become accustomed to "free" information. On the Internet there are few, if any, purely altruistic websites. Many of those active on the Internet are driven by motives that range from making a profit to proselytizing. There are also sites with much darker motives.

Writing on the leading Internet search provider, one commentator suggested that "the 'price' that we pay for Google's free services is to present ourselves as better targets for niche marketing".[3] Google, in common with most search engines, makes 99% of its profit from advertising. Of course, the better, more focused the advertising, the easier it is to sell. Companies, after all, don't want to spend money advertising to people who have no interest in their products.

Aside from the highly-targeted marketing based around social networks that we looked at in chapter four, an interesting development is the explosion of "how to" sites. They exist supposedly to explain everything, from how to tie a bow tie, to how to ride a unicycle. But for them, making money is equally interesting. Executives from these sites trawl daily though search results looking at what kinds of things people are looking for.[4] They then check to see how many "how to" videos or blogs are available on the Internet for these topics. When they find a

If It's Free, Then You Are The Product...

"hole in the market", they tender out for someone to create a "how to" video that covers the area of interest. People typically get paid a small amount for each video they submit. The final piece is to convince advertisers to pay the "how to" company for advertising. So, for example, if someone searches for "how to tie a bowtie", the web page displaying the video may also provide the viewer with a sponsored link to an online bowtie shop. Nothing is free.

Does It Matter?

"So what?" you may think. "Don't we already live in a society bombarded with advertising, from television, newspaper, radio, magazines and a myriad of other locations? There is nothing immoral or wrong about advertising. Is this not just another form of advertising that we have simply grown accustomed to ignoring?"

There is great strength in this argument, and I would not wish to suggest that advertising is immoral. After all, all kinds of people advertise, from political organizations, to companies wishing to sell a product, to churches advertising meetings and special events.

Some Dangers

Yet there are particular and very real dangers that stem from the appearance that the Internet seems impersonal. For example, as we've already seen, people are prone to reveal information about themselves on social networks, things that they would not say if they were face to face with an individual. This is information that can be used by advertisers or, if one is not careful, may even open the door for Internet predators. Take the case of a fifty-seven-year-old man, Colin Maddocks, who tricked twelve girls in British Columbia, Canada, between thirteen and sixteen years old into believing that he himself was a teenager. Virtual meetings would lead to face-to-face meetings where "Maddocks would offer alcohol, cigarettes and drugs as enticements in order to gain control and compliance to requests of a sexual nature."[5]

The truth is, that we are often far too naïve and ready to give out information about ourselves on a website, without knowing anything (or very little) about who runs the website, or what they will do with the

Chapter 7

information. Not only this, but even the information we search for provides data that can be sold.

INFORMATION FOR SALE

In his fascinating book entitled *Click—what millions of people are doing online and why it matters*[6] author Bill Tancer draws data from an Internet marketing company called *Hitwise Competitive Intelligence Services*. The data is a sample of over 10 million people using the Internet in the UK, USA and other countries (a small sample compared with most search engines). Tancer illustrates the power of information through a series of examples. In one graph he shows how searches for diet websites are at their highest two weeks after the US Thanksgiving holiday. Similarly, searches of homes for sale peak in July and then slowly decrease until just after Christmas when there is another significant jump of interest. All of this is useful information for anyone wishing to sell a diet or a home.

Another fascinating use of Internet data comes from the US Center for Disease Control (CDC). While attempting to track outbreaks of swine flu, the CDC turned to Google as a reliable source of information. The data provided by Google was as good as and more instantaneous than almost any other data source. Writing on their website, Google says that they "found that certain search terms are good indicators of flu activity.

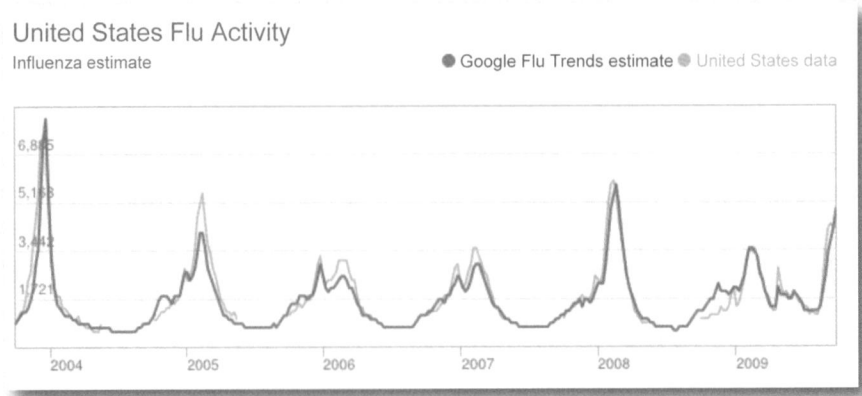

A comparison of 'Flu data from Google and the CDC

If It's Free, Then You Are The Product...

Google Flu Trends uses aggregated Google search data to estimate current flu activity around the world in near real-time."[7]

Author John Battelle, in his book *The Search—How Google and Its Rivals Rewrote the Rules of Business and Transformed Our Culture*[8] coins the term "the database of intention", which he describes as "the aggregate results of every search ever entered, every result list ever tendered, and every path taken as a result". He goes on to describe the power of Internet information by explaining that "information represents, in aggregate form, a place holder for the intentions of humankind—a massive database of desires, needs, wants, and likes that can be discovered, subpoenaed, archived, tracked, and exploited to all sorts of ends. Such a beast has never before existed in the history of culture, but is almost guaranteed to grow exponentially from this day forward."

KEEPING TRACK OF YOUR LOCATION

The amount of information being made available about us is hard to imagine—from tracking cookies stored on a computer browser, to a record of every search that we have made online. In April 2011, both Apple and Google admitted that they collected and stored location

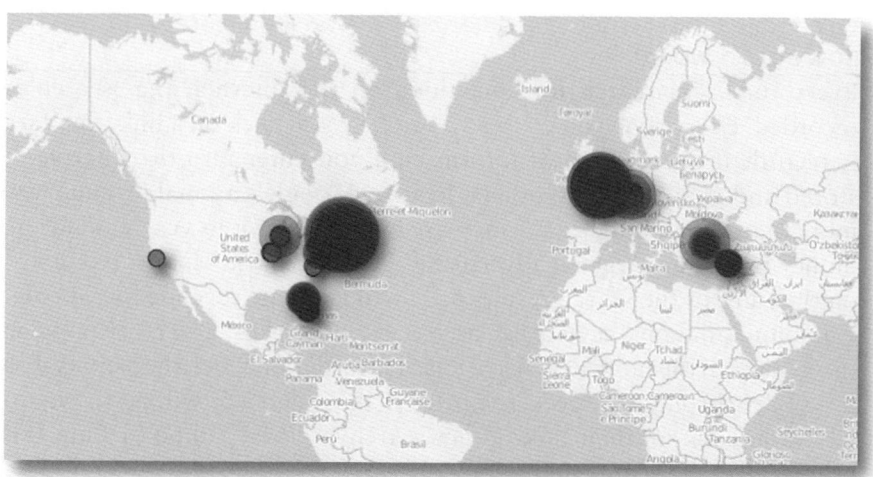

The author's travel locations in the past year—extracted from an iPhone

You, Your Family and the Internet **61**

Chapter 7

information from mobile devices such as the hugely popular iPhone and Android-based phones. This revelation created a controversy that quickly escalated to the US Congress. While both companies explained that none of this information was being passed on to anyone else, and that it was all recorded in an anonymous fashion, this disclosure worried many about what might be possible. The two security researchers that uncovered the problem also wrote a program to display location information that had been stored in Apple's iTunes backups.

GOING VIRAL

Internet marketers sell information, and the more targeted it is the better. It has been noted that "Eighty-nine percent of adults share content with friends, family and associates."[9] Viral marketing works by adding targeted advertising to content that might be shared—for example a *YouTube* video, or a joke email. The psychology behind viral marketing is subtle. People receiving email, or a recommendation from a friend or colleague, are less likely to discard it. One viral marketer explains that "people generally like to share content because it makes them feel more important. If you appear to be the first to find something of interest to your peers or others and then give that thing to them, it will gain you kudos and instill within you a subtle sense of increased social worth."[10]

HOW DOES IT WORK?

Every time you search for something on the Internet, that search is recorded. Every time you go to a website, or you click on a link, that fact is recorded. Every piece of information you enter into the Internet is stored and may be sold to others. In 2010, Google's annual revenue was more than $29 billion, a 24% increase over the previous year. It made its money by selling targeted advertising. Clicking those "sponsored links" on the right of the search results page will generate revenue for Google. Companies bid on "keywords" used during searches. The more popular the keyword, the more expensive it is. The order in which the "sponsored links" are displayed reflects the price that bidders are willing to pay to have you click on their link. Other search engines, Yahoo or Bing and others, all operate on a similar model.

If It's Free, Then You Are The Product...

Some sample information from Google Analytics showing which country and which town in the UK website visitors came from

Website owners have a similar array of tools at their disposal. These tools, called "analytics", store and analyze every piece of information—the number of visitors, where they come from, how long they spent browsing the website, which pages they looked at, whether they entered the website as a result of a search or from clicking a link on another website, what page they exited the website at, etc. All this information is useful in targeting users, improving the website and better selling the products on display.

Some Key Principles

It should be apparent by now that everything we do on the Internet is being recorded, catalogued, organized and probably sold. In one sense, there is very little we can do about this if we are to use the Internet at all. By giving away this information, we are essentially paying for the creation and the upkeep of the websites that we use.

However, a key Christian principle to remember is that we are to be wise about the world we live in and not to be easily taken in. Christians are to be meek, but not naïve. The Bible puts it this way: "We should no longer be children, tossed to and fro and carried about with every wind of doctrine, by the trickery of men, in the cunning craftiness of deceitful plotting" (Ephesians 4:14). Again, the Bible explains that we are sent

Chapter 7

forth "as sheep in the midst of wolves" and must therefore be "wise as serpents, and harmless as doves" (Matthew 10:16). The injunction comes in the context of a warning to "beware of men, for they will deliver you up to councils ..." Information gleaned on the Internet, particularly social networks, is already being used as evidence in the courts. Now, imagine the situation in which the law of the land was anti-Christian—something countries like the UK have come very close to with efforts to introduce "equality legislation". How might the information that is harvested about us on the Internet be used in such an instance? While we have liberty, we are not to be shy in using our rights where they can further the cause of the gospel, as Paul did when confronting the authorities in Philippi after his release from prison (Acts 25:11). But in all things, it is good to remember and understand people's motives and the potential use that they can make of information that we have freely given away on the Internet.

Practical Advice
When George Orwell described "Big Brother" in his novel entitled *1984*, he had no idea of the extent to which our every action would be catalogued. While it is possible to install software that claims to cover up our tracks when browsing, in reality, this is a very difficult thing to achieve. Rather, we should be very wary of giving out personal information, particularly to websites of which we know very little. We must always bear in mind that the "privacy of our own home" is a misnomer when it comes to the Internet and that everything that we do is being recorded. Let us be wise in what we give away, and the information we post, employing that most uncommon quality of "common sense".

At a minimum, we should install good antivirus and spyware software, make sure that the software is kept up to date and that we use it to scan our computers on a regular basis. Also make sure that the software supports an "auto-protect" mode in which our activity is constantly being monitored for potential threats. Most modern antivirus packages support all of these features.

Finally, let us not be naïve. Whenever we visit any website, our first questions should be, "Why did someone go to the effort of creating this

If It's Free, Then You Are The Product...

website?" and "How do they make their money?" Understanding the motives behind the website is the key to being able to make the decision on whether to continue using a website, or to enter any personal information.

For Discussion

Please read Mathew 5:5, 2 Corinthians 10:1 and Colossians 3:12. The Lord Jesus is described as meek, yet in John 2:15 he is seen driving out merchants from the temple with a whip. As Christians, we are clearly called to be meek. But how does this differ from naïvety?

Please read Daniel 1:1–16 and Matthew 5:13–14, 10:16. Should we avoid using the Internet altogether for fear of identify theft, being taken in by phishing[11] or having our information used in ways that we did not wish or anticipate?

Notes

1. googleblog.blogspot.com/2008/07/we-knew-web-was-big.html
2. www.pcpro.co.uk/features/110472/whos-the-biggest-threat-to-your-identity-you
3. www.pcpro.co.uk/features/110472/whos-the-biggest-threat-to-your-identity-you
4. Google Trends, along with others, provide statistics of what people are searching for.
5. www.vancouverite.com/2009/12/08/12-kelowna-school-girls-lured-on-internet-with-drugs-smokes-and-booze/
6. **Tancer, Bill,** *Click: What Millions of People Are Doing Online and Why It Matters* (New York: Hyperion Press, 2008).
7. www.google.org/about/flutrends/how.html
8. **Battelle, John,** *The Search—How Google and Its Rivals Rewrote the Rules of Business and Transformed Our Culture* (Penguin Books, 2005)
9. www.justilien.com/research/viral-link-baiting.htm
10. How Users Share Viral Content Online, www.viralmanager.com/strategy
11. Phishing is a form of email fraud. Criminals create emails and websites that closely resemble those of legitimate companies. Their goal is to entice you to provide them with personal information they can then use to gain access to your assets or other sensitive data—from www.jpmorgan.com/tss/General/What_is_Phishing_/1143727608561

Chapter 8

Internet Games

I remember programming my first game using a Teletype and punch tape for storage around 1977. It was a version of the then popular *Mastermind* game and ran on a computer that filled a big room and required a large number of people to keep it going. But it was very exciting for a seventeen-year-old at the time. Today, a hand-held smart phone has more power, and significantly more memory capacity, than this venerable relic.

A state-of-the-art 'teletype', circa 1977! A nice 'trick' was to try to print out your name using the punch tape on the left of the teletype!

A few years later, while I carried out postgraduate study into the uses of Artificial Intelligence, the height of research included developing software versions of the game of chess. One interesting program, called ELIZA, sought to simulate a Rogerian psychotherapist. ELIZA mostly rephrased the user's statements as questions and posed those back to the "patient". For example, ELIZA might respond to "My head hurts," with "Why do you say your head hurts?" The response to "My mother hates me," would be "Who else in your family hates you?"[1]

Ping Pong

By the mid 1970s, games started appearing for the home, the most memorable of which was the game of PONG, a computer version of Ping-Pong.

Things developed rapidly and were

spurred along with advances such as the Sinclair ZX80 in the UK and later the Spectrum computers. By the mid 1980s, games were gaining a foothold in people's homes with some 20,000 titles (mostly games) having been released for the Spectrum. Some concern was already being expressed about the time that children were spending playing computer games, though, at the time, other non-computer games such as *Dungeons and Dragons* were still just as popular, and no less controversial. The concern was not only with the depiction of witchcraft in such games, but also with role-playing described as games "in which the protagonists create and control the actions of a cast of characters."[2]

Fast-forward Thirty Years

Thirty or more years later, gaming technology has progressed beyond recognition. Today's games involve lifelike realism of 3D computer generated environments. The best selling game "World of Warcraft" involves realistic battle action in a multi-player scenario with hundreds of thousands of simultaneous users joining in from around the world (though each game may only have a few dozen players). From modest beginnings, worldwide sales of games are now estimated at $50B (£33B) and are expected to grow to nearly $100B by 2015.[3] In the US, 68% of households own video games, with an average "gamer" spending eighteen hours a week playing. Interestingly, the average age for a gamer is thirty-five, of which 60% are male.[4] Games come in all shapes and sizes, and now include parental ratings—from "suitable for everyone" to "mature themes". One example of a game with "mature themes", based on Dante's *Inferno*, allows users to explore all nine levels of hell. One gamer said that he "loved the voice of Lucifer".

Gaming Communities

Many games now require users to join teams. Winning teams are those most effective in developing strategies and cooperation between players. In other words, they require the same type of real life skills that are found in industry (or on the battlefield). Some game consoles, such as the highly successful Nintendo Wii, have opened up a new world of opportunities. Families get together to play games of "tennis" against

Chapter 8

each other. Millions of people have purchased the "Wii Fit" to help them loose weight. Game consoles have even been installed in nursing homes to allow residents to challenge others over the Internet at bowling.

While "serious" gamers may sneer at the seeming simplicity of the Wii, another online phenomenon has been the arrival of massively popular Facebook games. Within months of its introduction, an estimated 30 million people played the game "Farmville" every day.[5] Zynga, a startup founded in 2007, creator of Farmville and other games such as "Mafia Wars", claims to have more than 100 million unique monthly users for its social games on Facebook. All of its games are simple two-dimensional titles that are popular because friends can play them with each other. Commenting on "Mafia Wars", *Time* magazine explained that "you don't play Mafia Wars alone. Your friends on Facebook who also play Mafia Wars make up your family. They help you with your business and fight with you and send you gifts. The bigger the family, the better for business." The same is true with Farmville, a game in which players plant and grow crops, on a virtual farm surrounded by virtual neighbors that are also Facebook "friends". The games cost nothing, though players can purchase things with real money if they want to speed things along. It is clear, therefore, that some games can have beneficial effects, providing much-needed relaxation and developing skills of strategy or coordination.

The Psychological Impact of Games

There is also a dark side to gaming. Not only are some games clearly inappropriate irrespective of age, others can induce compulsive or addictive behavior in some people. The world's first game addiction clinic opened in Amsterdam in July 2006.[6] There is also the much-studied question of the impact of violent games on children and adults. A study by the American Psychological Association concluded that "fantasy violence is often perceived (incorrectly) by parents and public policy-makers as safe even for children. However, experimental studies with college students have consistently found increased aggression after exposure to clearly unrealistic and fantasy-violent video games. Indeed,

Internet Games

at least one recent study found significant increases in aggression by college students after playing E-rated (suitable for everyone) violent video games."[7] Another study concluded that "playing video games may increase aggressive behavior because violent acts are continually repeated throughout the video game."[8]

One expert in the field is Dr. Orzack, a licensed clinical psychologist, a founder of the Computer Addiction Service and a member of the Harvard Medical School faculty. She compares computer gaming addiction to gambling addiction and suggests that 40% of World of Warcraft players are addicted[9]—a suggestion that brought about strong reaction, both positive and negative. One such reaction comes from a distressed wife who says of her husband that "he rushes back home every day to play such games from 7pm till 2am ... When I try to talk to him he can't be bothered to pay attention."[10]

Dr. Orzack provides some fascinating insights into the symptoms of game addictions, which she explains are "quite specific":[11]

Psychological Symptoms
- Having a sense of well-being or euphoria while at the computer
- Inability to stop the activity
- Craving more and more time at the computer
- Neglect of family and friends
- Feeling empty, depressed, irritable when not at the computer
- Lying to employers and family about activities
- Problems with school or job

Physical Symptoms
- Carpal tunnel syndrome
- Dry eyes
- Migraine headaches
- Back aches
- Eating irregularities, such as skipping meals
- Failure to attend to personal hygiene
- Sleep disturbances, change in sleep pattern

It should also be noted that a number of these symptoms (particularly the

Chapter 8

physical ones) may arise naturally from the work that many people do, which may often require them to use a computer for most of the working day.

Key Principles
There is no doubt that we (whether adults or children) should stay away from games that promote gratuitous violence or sexual themes. These are simply inappropriate. It should also be noted that the Bible, particularly the Old Testament, is full of violence. Some of this violence is sanctioned by God himself, and, at times, described in excruciating detail.[12] However, violence in Scripture is always there for a reason. 2 Timothy 3:16 explains that all Scripture is "profitable for doctrine, for reproof, for correction, for instruction in righteousness". Sometimes we find it hard to understand certain things that are clearly portrayed in the Bible. However, that does not mean that they are not true, and that they are not written for a specific purpose. What is certain is that, unlike online games, violence in the Bible is never there to entertain us.

We would also do well to remember that children often do not see things the same way as adults do, seeing only the game rather than the more sinister side that may be portrayed. If our children spend what we consider to be inordinate time playing online games, we should also remember that what we may think of as an addiction in our children may be no more than a normal passing fad, part of a normal developmental process and something that they will naturally grow out of.

Nonetheless, there are real dangers. One study speaks of games blurring "the boundaries between reality and fantasy, leading people to engage in immoral or anti-social activities, or ... leading young people to Paganism or Satanism."[13] Another study for the Centers for Disease Control published in the American Journal of Preventive Medicine found, among adult gamers, "a higher BMI (increased weight problems) and a greater number of poor mental-health days" as well as other negative physical and mental health issues.[14]

A key principle is, therefore, that of self-control. As we have seen, it is possible to be drawn into online gaming and to loose all sense of time, to become anti-social and not to do the things we ought to do. The Bible speaks of self-control as the "fruit of the Spirit" (Galatians 5:23), something that is developed through the Holy Spirit working in the life of a believer (2 Peter 1:6, Acts 24:25). Our inability to control our urges and to be drawn in by gaming (and other activities) on the Internet is a sin of commission—that is, something we do.

The flipside of this is the sin of omission—namely something that we do not do, even though we ought to. Ephesians 5:16 speaks of "redeeming the time, because the days are evil". The Lord Jesus Christ was supremely focused on his mission. "Moderation in all things" is in fact a very important motto. While online gaming may be a legitimate form of relaxation, let us not get drawn into it in such a way that we cannot stop, and we fail to take part in more important activities.

These principles will become increasingly important in the future as games become much more immersive, blurring the line between fiction and reality. Leading the way is Microsoft with its best-selling game controller—the Kinect—which at one point was the fastest selling consumer device in history. While the Wii remote is able to sense movement and position, the Kinect has taken this to a much higher level. The Kinect combines cameras, 3D (three dimensional) depth perception as well as voice and facial recognition to be able to capture the motion of up to forty joints in the human body, all without the need for a controller. The Kinect first came to public attention when it was still called "Project Natal". In an online demonstration,[15] a subject could be seen interacting with a computer as if it were another person, even "passing" a drawing over to the computer to have it comment on it. Milo, a fictitious digital "being", would recognize people's faces and voices, and then have a "conversation", sensing emotions and responding in kind. Where the Kinect takes us is anyone's guess. Enterprising and creative software engineers are bound to exploit this technology in ways the original creators never considered—good and bad.

While the technology may be exciting, we need to be ever vigilant. Not only should we take care that we do not get absorbed into unreality, into a virtual world that seems better than the one we live in, we must also understand that, for many people, this kind of escapism is a new drug, one that they cannot do without.

Chapter 8

A virtual 'chat room' based on the Kinect, where participants can "see" each other and even have their avatar reflect their own facial expressions and body movements.[16]

Practical Advice

We need to remember that gaming is much like other leisure activities such as watching television or going to the movies. All of these come with dangers and require self-discipline. There are three specific practical steps that we can take, particularly with respect to children:

1. We should pay attention to labels. Games, like movies, often come with ratings. These should be read and considered. If, for example, a game is rated as "AO" (Adults Only), it is because it has "content that should only be played by persons eighteen years and older" and that "may include prolonged scenes of intense violence and/or graphic sexual content and nudity."[17]

2. We should know what our children play. Placing a game console or computer in an open area rather than allowing children to play in their rooms is always wise. Better still, we could play the game with the child. Game consoles such as the Wii encourage family participation. This will turn gaming from a negative "You can't do that" into something positive that you can all do together.

3. We should set time limits. This applies to both adults and children. Setting a time limit on recreational activity (of any sort) is always a good principle, particularly with children and teenagers in which the ability to exercise self-control is still developing.

For Discussion

Please read Ephesians 5:15–21, Matthew 14:23 and Exodus 20:8–11. Managing our time is clearly important in the Bible, though we can also see that it is important to have time to "recharge our batteries". Where do you think the balance lies between leisure and work? How much time should Christians devote to themselves (relaxation) rather than worthwhile activity (outside of work)?

Please read 1 Peter 4:1–4. Roman games, at the time of Christ, were notorious for their violence, with many Christians suffering martyrdom in the arena. Similarly, some Roman practices involved very loose moral behavior. Are we in danger of recreating these "pastimes" using the Internet?

Notes

1 A good description of ELIZA can be found at en.wikipedia.org/wiki/ELIZA
2 This quote comes from a 2005 paper published in the Journal of Religion and Popular Culture
3 vgsales.wikia.com/wiki/video_game_industry
4 From the publication "Essential facts about the computer and video game industry, 2009, Entertainment Software Association"
5 venturebeat.com/2009/11/23/zynga-crosses-100-million-users-and-expands-beyond-facebook-games/.
6 *Video Addiction* by Laura Parker, GameSpot www.gamespot.com
7 Violent Video Games: Myths, Facts, and Unanswered Questions, by **Dr. Craig A Anderson,** Psychological Science Agenda, Science Briefs, Oct 2003
8 Gentile, D. A. & **Anderson, C. A.** (2003). Violent video games: The newest media violence hazard. In **D. A. Gentile** (Ed.), Media violence and children. Westport, CT: Praeger Publishing. Quoted in www.pamf.org/preteen/parents/videogames.html
9 arstechnica.com/old/content/2006/08/7459.ars
10 Quoted on a Facebook group—
www.facebook.com/group.php?gid=72742847955#!/group.php?gid=72742847955&v=wall

Chapter 8

11 www.computeraddiction.com/

12 For example see Judges 3:21-22, 4:21, Deuteronomy 2:34

13 Role-Playing Games and the Christian Right: Community Formation in Response to a Moral Panic, **David Waldron,** Journal of Religion and Popular Culture Vol 9, Spring 2005

14 "Health-Risk Correlates of Video-Game Playing Among Adults" *by James B Weaver III,* et al., *American Journal of Preventive Medicine,* Volume 37, Issue 4 (October 2009)

15 See www.youtube.com/watch?v=g_txF7iETX0 and www.youtube.com/watch?v=2g_U02Pz0P4

16 Image from www.microft.com—Copyright notice: MICROSOFT AND/OR ITS RESPECTIVE SUPPLIERS MAKE NO REPRESENTATIONS ABOUT THE SUITABILITY OF THE INFORMATION CONTAINED IN THE DOCUMENTS AND RELATED GRAPHICS PUBLISHED AS PART OF THE SERVICES FOR ANY PURPOSE. ALL SUCH DOCUMENTS AND RELATED GRAPHICS ARE PROVIDED "AS IS" WITHOUT WARRANTY OF ANY KIND. MICROSOFT AND/OR ITS RESPECTIVE SUPPLIERS HEREBY DISCLAIM ALL WARRANTIES AND CONDITIONS WITH REGARD TO THIS INFORMATION, INCLUDING ALL WARRANTIES AND CONDITIONS OF MERCHANTABILITY, WHETHER EXPRESS, IMPLIED OR STATUTORY, FITNESS FOR A PARTICULAR PURPOSE, TITLE AND NON-INFRINGEMENT. IN NO EVENT SHALL MICROSOFT AND/OR ITS RESPECTIVE SUPPLIERS BE LIABLE FOR ANY SPECIAL, INDIRECT OR CONSEQUENTIAL DAMAGES OR ANY DAMAGES WHATSOEVER RESULTING FROM LOSS OF USE, DATA OR PROFITS, WHETHER IN AN ACTION OF CONTRACT, NEGLIGENCE OR OTHER TORTIOUS ACTION, ARISING OUT OF OR IN CONNECTION WITH THE USE OR PERFORMANCE OF INFORMATION AVAILABLE FROM THE SERVICES.

THE DOCUMENTS AND RELATED GRAPHICS PUBLISHED ON THE SERVICES COULD INCLUDE TECHNICAL INACCURACIES OR TYPOGRAPHICAL ERRORS. CHANGES ARE PERIODICALLY ADDED TO THE INFORMATION HEREIN. MICROSOFT AND/OR ITS RESPECTIVE SUPPLIERS MAY MAKE IMPROVEMENTS AND/OR CHANGES IN THE PRODUCT(S) AND/OR THE PROGRAM(S) DESCRIBED HEREIN AT ANY TIME.

17 Rating definitions can be found at the "Entertainment Software Rating Board" website—www.esrb.org/ratings/ratings_guide.jsp

Chapter 9

Internet Gambling

Online gambling is all about making money—a lot of money. While statistics are difficult to find, since much of what happens online is unregulated, one estimate suggests revenues of $27B (£17B) worldwide in 2009 rising to $36B (£22B) by 2012.¹ That is more than the Gross Domestic Product (GDP) of 70% of the countries in the world.² In Europe, online gambling alone (about 8% of all gambling) is predicted to generate $18B (£11B) by 2012. So much money is involved that governments around the world have been trying to find ways of getting their share by legitimizing gambling in order to generate tax income. Every day some 2 million people deposit additional funds into their online gambling account. The US State of Iowa, keen to capitalize on gambling revenue (estimated at $80M (£50M) per year), justified setting up an online poker site by suggesting that it "would allow them to provide a safe online poker environment for their citizens."³ Several commentators have noted that governments seem to be addicted to gambling revenue, one newspaper going as far as accusing the Canadian government of "fueling the spread of a destructive disease".⁴ In the USA, one organization which ironically calls itself "the safe and secure Internet gambling initiative" claimed that taxation from regulated Internet gambling would raise nearly $42 billion over ten years in new revenue which would help Congress "pay for health care reform and other critical programs".⁵

Gambling Odds

While some people gamble out of desperation and others see it as a form of entertainment, it is not unreasonable to suggest that people gamble, whether online or not, because they have an expectation, or, at the very least, a hope, of winning. But the odds of winning are always against the gambler in favor of the house. The odds of winning at national or state lotteries are smoothly passed over by those who run these games—often government sponsored—as they raise considerable sums of money in a kind of "stealth tax". While lottery advertising claims that "someone

Chapter 9

must win", simple mathematics quickly show that the chance of winning is astronomical.[6] The likelihood of wining the British Jackpot lottery is estimated at around 1 in 14 million.[7] In contrast, the chance of being struck by lightning is 1 in 2 million; of a woman giving birth to quadruplets, 1 in 705 thousand. And that is to say nothing of the chance of being killed in a car crash: 1 in 5 thousand![8]

Professor Tyler Jarvis, chair of the Department of Mathematics at Brigham Young University in the US State of Utah, has contributed to several academic papers on the odds at gambling. He writes:

> Almost everyone has trouble understanding the huge and tiny numbers involved in gambling odds. But learning about these odds has convinced many people that gambling is not the harmless pastime they thought it was. The main thing to understand is that the odds always favor the house. For example, the house's take on a slot machine can be as high as 35%. This means that if you bet ten dollars, you can expect to walk away with only $6.50; if you bet $100, you can expect to keep only $65, and so forth. The more you play, the more you lose. Although some gamblers are ahead temporarily, in the long run the odds will prevail, and the gambler will lose.[9]

A Cornucopia of Choice

Almost every form of gambling is available online—from betting on a large number of sports, to online casinos, lottery, bingo, blackjack, poker, and so on. Author Mark Balestra, in his book entitled *The Complete Idiot's Guide to Online Gambling*, waxes eloquent about the delights (as he sees them) of online gambling:

> This is gambling like you've never experienced it before. Could you have imagined that hundreds of casinos, several dozen horse racing tracks, and a handful of bingo halls could be folded neatly into a box small enough to be carried in a briefcase? That's right, casinos, lotteries, sports books, racetracks, and bingo halls from all over the world are at your fingertips 24-hours-a-day.[10]

Why Do People Do It?

In a BBC web forum, gamblers past and present speak of the lure of gambling. "Dan", from Peterborough in England, explains that he is a "recovering compulsive gambler" and that "a lot more people have a gambling addiction than actually realize it. I didn't realize I had a gambling problem until it had destroyed my life. I nearly lost my job; I did lose my car; I nearly lost my girlfriend and my family didn't really want to talk to me. I was a total waste of space."[11]

A scholarly paper[12] on the impact of Internet gambling warns that "the proliferation of online casinos raises fears that the social harms of gambling will spread exponentially because of easy access and an inability to regulate Internet activity. Among these societal harms are addiction and problem gambling, access by minors, consumer vulnerability to fraud, and criminal activity. Gambling is addictive ... Youth are particularly vulnerable to addiction. Unlike brick-and-mortar casinos, Internet gaming sites have no reasonable means of verifying age at the door; therefore, minors have an easier time accessing gambling."

In a letter to the US Congress, the organization *Focus on the Family*[13] warned that "the prevalence of gambling addiction is three to four times higher with Internet gambling versus non-Internet gambling. When all factors are considered—24/7 availability, in-home accessibility, speed of play, secrecy, anonymity, extremely addictive, no real age verification—online gambling represents a highly invasive and reckless form of taxation dependent on human exploitation."

Relaying her tragic story of addiction to Internet poker,[14] "Jane" explains that "even though we only had £20 a week for food, I was spending £100 a day gambling on my credit card while [my husband] was at work. I knew it was wrong to beg him for money whilst spending so much on Internet poker, but I just couldn't stop." She goes on to explain some of the allure of online gambling: "With Internet gambling, you can just click a button and money is transferred into your account, but the money slips away really quickly ... Online anyone can gamble. I know of fifteen-year-olds who play on their dads' accounts. It's really easy to bet with money you can't see, and you can lose £1,000 in a night."

A Darker Side ...

Gambling is not only psychologically destructive, but it can also have a very dark criminal side. Writing in the International Journal of criminal

Chapter 9

justice Sciences,[15] Wojciech Filipkowski from the Faculty of Law, University of Białystok, Poland says:

> Internet gambling has been identified—by experts in the field of money laundering and tax evasion—as a potentially ideal web-based service to legitimize ill-gotten gains. In the real world casinos are used to launder dirty money. The same thing can be done by on-line gambling sites. There are two possibilities: launderer exploits legitimate web-based service or launderer sets up an on-line gambling company in order to clean money.

Because many online gambling websites are located in off-shore financial centers that lack regulatory or prudential measures, money is taken from gamblers through legitimate credit cards, and paid as "winnings" from unregulated accounts based on income from illegitimate activities such as theft, drug-sales or prostitution. In this way, dirty money is laundered into the system as legitimate winnings.

Key Principles

Gambling is a difficult area for many. Some believe with passion that no form of "chance" should ever be part of normal life. In this instance, all forms of chance are deemed inappropriate, whether gambling, lotteries or even the stock market. Others take a somewhat different view, believing that a little money spent on games of chance is no worse than paying for many forms of entertainment, provided there is no expectation of a return. They see little wrong with the thrill of "taking a chance", something, it is claimed, that businesses do every day. One should hasten to add that while businesses do indeed take risks, these are usually taken after much consideration and with the expectation of a solid return. This cannot be said of gambling, an activity carefully devised so that the "house never looses". The fact is that gambling is not like any other "risk" and is definitely not an investment. The advent of online gambling has taken this to a new level by providing an easy-to-use, always available, and totally addictive activity to users across the world in the "comfort of their own homes".

The Bible lays down key principles that must be observed:

Internet Gambling

- A man should work for a living—"If anyone will not work, neither shall he eat" (2 Thessalonians 3:10). Sadly, gambling can easily become the last resort of the desperate, a way out for someone who might have got into a tricky financial situation. In contrast, the Christian work ethic is clear. We work for a living, we spend within our means, and we do not squander our money on things like gambling.
- Greed is always wrong—it comes from a corrupt heart (Mark 7:22–23, Luke 11:39) and is a sin. It eats people up. They can never have enough. Greed is what brought down the financial markets towards the end of the first decade of the twenty-first century as speculators played the markets with other peoples' money. Gambling of any sort encourages greed, wanting more than we have been given by God, and, worse of all, without any effort on our part.
- Addiction to anything is wrong. The Bible speaks of Christian virtues such as sober-mindedness (1 Timothy 3:2), temperance (Titus 2:2) and self-control (Galatians 5:23). In contrast, any addiction is wrong—our lives are to be lived for the glory of God, not to be squandered. Time is the one preeminent and precious commodity which, once gone, can never be recovered. Online gambling sites are geared towards addicting users, drawing them in with enticements of winning. This is especially concerning because of a lack of regulation and age verification. The young and the easily swayed are particularly vulnerable.

Practical Advice

The best practical advice that I can offer is to stay away. Gambling, and in particular online gambling, offers real dangers. Such activities can ruin lives, draw people away from legitimate undertakings, isolate them, and bring despair, financial difficulties and addiction. On top of it all, because online gambling is so unregulated, it is possible that money spent and received has been tied to organized crime.

In Chapter six on pornography, we explored the use of accountability websites. As with other forms of addiction, an accountability partner is a good idea for those who are drawn to online gambling.

Chapter 9

Blocking the gambling sites is also advisable. There are several ways of doing this. Many modern Internet broadband modems (or routers) offer filters that can block gambling sites. Software can also be installed on each computer you use—many of the modern antivirus software packages now bundle firewalls and filters. These filters can be set up so that they are password-protected. This allows parents to prevent children from accessing undesirable sites. A word of warning here—there are ways around the password schemes, but they require some significant technical knowledge. However, since teenagers tend to share this knowledge, it is always best to change passwords on a regular basis.

For Discussion

Please read 1 Timothy 3:8 (the words "not given to" can also be translated "not addicted to), 1 Corinthians 16:15 (the Greek word *tas'-so* which is translated as "devoted", can also be translated as "addicted"). Any addiction is not biblical and can also be destructive. Why is gambling addictive? What are the dangers we need to look out for to avoid becoming addicted, even to legitimate things?

Please read Colossians 3:11–13, 2 Thessalonians 3:13–15 and 1 Corinthians 10:12. What principles can we apply to helping people who are facing addiction?

Notes

1 From www.h2gc.com
2 Taken from www.nationmaster.com/
3 pokernewsboy.com/legal-poker-news/online-poker-to-give-iowa-80-million/2172
4 *The National Post*, 1 November 2008
5 www.safeandsecureig.org/news/press_releases/09-10-29_TaxScore.html. Also quoted at www.prnewswire.com/news-releases/joint-committee-on-taxation-projects-internet-gambling-regulation-would-generate-nearly-42-billion-in-new-revenue-67209607.html
6 The following website can be used to calculate the odds of your wining your local lottery—webmath.com/lottery.html
7 lottery.merseyworld.com/Info/Chances.html
8 www.webspawner.com/users/maddo1029/
9 Gambling: What are the Odds? Found at www.math.byu.edu/~jarvis/gambling.html

Internet Gambling

10 *The Complete Idiot's Guide to Online Gambling,* **Mark Balestra,** Publisher: Alpha Books, 2000—page 5.
11 newsforums.bbc.co.uk
12 www.law.northwestern.edu/journals/njtip/v7/n2/2/#note*
13 fota.cdnetworks.net/pdfs/2009-06-04-gambling-letter.pdf
14 www.thesite.org/community/reallife/truestories/internetpokerruinedmylifex
15 Vol 3 Issue 1 January–June 2008

Chapter 10

News and Views

On Tuesday April 16, 1912 the *London Times* reported that "the White Star liner *Titanic*, which left Southampton on Wednesday [April 10] on her maiden voyage to New York, came into collision with an iceberg some distance from Cape Race, Newfoundland, late on Sunday night, and sank yesterday morning. It is feared that only 675 of the passengers and crew, who numbered 2,300, have been saved."

The following week, on April 23, the front page of the same newspaper carried an artist's impression with the following caption:

An ocean disaster, unprecedented in history, has happened in the Atlantic. The White Star liner Titanic, on her maiden voyage, carrying nearly 2,400 people, has been lost near Cape Race[1]

That was big news, and the information, relayed by telegraph, was

82 You, Your Family and the Internet

printed within a day of the event taking place. Commenting in the same issue, the editor noted that "the disaster ... is a forcible reminder of the existence of natural forces which from time to time upset all our calculations and baffle all our precautions."

Writing some seventy years earlier, on October 15, 1842, the same newspaper carried a report relaying the "most disastrous news ... from the interior [of India], where the 41st Regiment had been cut to pieces". The incident took place in August 1842, and the news had taken nearly two months to reach London.

In June 2009, Iranians took to the streets to protest what they saw as rigged elections. News was reported minute by minute, as it unfolded, by protesters sending tweets.[2] People across the world followed these events in real time. Someone calling himself "Montris" sent the following tweet[3]

> Govt buildings being smashed, police batoning protesters, tear gas, rocks ... head wounds all around Tehran

Later that day, another protester reported on twitter:

> Between 50–100 dead. Police on motorcycles beating people. They drive by attacking women

Protesters posted videos on YouTube directly from their Smartphones. One of the most harrowing of these videos was that of girl of twenty dying in the streets after being shot during a demonstration. The video was instantly available across the web and was watched by tens of thousands, as well as being broadcast by television stations.

Social Media, Riots and the Middle East

The Spring of 2011 saw widespread popular uprising and disturbances in the Middle East. Beginning in Tunisia, these popular movements led to widespread change in countries such as Algeria, Egypt, Libya, Jordan, Yemen, Sudan and others.

There is little doubt that Social Media was a key enabler for these protests with Sites such as Facebook and Twitter being used to help

Chapter 10

coordinate and inform people directly without any intermediary or censorship. Videos posted to YouTube were also seized by the world's media as evidence of what was "really going on" on the streets of these troubled countries.

Jillian York of Harvard University's Berkman Center for Internet and Society commented, "For the past few days, I have been watching people on Twitter ... I have also seen things such as "Google docs" literally laying out plans for protests. And so in this case, I have seen a lot more public organization on the Internet."4

Even in the West, Facebook has been used to incite riots. In the UK, the summer of 2011 saw some terrible scenes of rioting and looting. In August of that year, two individuals (Perry Sutcliffe, 22, and Jordan Blackshaw, 20) were jailed for four years for urging other to riots by posting on their Facebook pages.

On the other hand, politicians have been quick to see the Internet as a means to bring democracy directly to the people. US Secretary of State Hilary Clinton, in a 2010 speech, stated that "we will work with partners in industry, academia, and nongovernmental organizations to establish a standing effort that will harness the power of connection technologies and apply them to our diplomatic goals."5

To counter these grand designs, author Evgeny Morozov, in his acclaimed book *The Net Delusion*, explains that Clinton's goal to "put these tools in the hands of people around the world who will use them to advance democracy and human rights" is naïve. Morozov continues: "The most popular Internet searches on Russian search engines are not for 'What is democracy?' or 'How to protect human rights' but for 'What is love?' and 'How to lose weight.' "6

To some, the kind of popular uprising seen in countries across the Middle East would have been impossible without social media. To others, social media was just a small part of the picture and one of the tools that happened to be available.

In a debate sponsored by the Open Society Foundations, the participants argued that social media tended to make reporters lazy, tempting them to use easily available information rather than looking deeper into issues. Citing as an example the disturbances in the Middle

East, they explained that these didn't happen just because people created a Facebook page but originated in a social and cultural context after years of oppression.7

The iPad and the Age of 24/7

In April of 2010, eBay founder and Hawaii resident, Pierre Omidyar, started a new kind of newspaper called *Civil Beat*. At its inception, the editor, a man by the name of John Temple, explained, "We're going to be sharing with the public what we're working on as we're working on it, and the experience of working on it". In other words, reporters will keep blogs and send tweets as they pursue stories. They'll write regular news articles but they'll also host online discussions of the beats they cover—like politics or education. And they'll maintain so-called topic pages which will act as a constant living story that is continually updated.8

While launching the iPad, the late Steve Jobs of Apple demonstrated how the way that we read news is changing. Traditional newspapers such as the *New York Times* and *USA Today* soon launched iPad versions to allow users to subscribe to the latest news stories over the Internet. The media mogul Rupert Murdoch called this a "digital renaissance" when he launched a newspaper specifically designed for the new media called *The Daily*, its main selling point being the instant availability of "High definition video, 360-degree photographs, text stories interlaced with Twitter feeds and a 100 pages of current events, gossip, sports, apps and games delivered daily."9 According to Murdoch, "New times demand new journalism." But by the end 2011, *The Daily* had failed to attract enough readers to break even (it had only a sixth of what it needed according to the *Guardian*)10 but the ideas behind online news are already catching on. Imagine being able not only to read news, but also to be instantly linked to a video posted by a blogger on the web or having the ability to customize a newspaper so that it fits your particular interests.

The news is becoming a commodity. It's something that we can tailor to reflect our tastes and interests. It's a means not only of receiving stories from around the world, but of instantly being kept up to date. And it gives us the opportunity to interact with people in the news via email, twitter, instant messengers or web discussions. We no longer need to be

Chapter 10

passive recipients of news; we can now provide feedback, opinions and complete instant surveys.

News as Entertainment

So why does this matter? In his well-known book *Amusing ourselves to death*,[11] the late Neil Postman, a professor of Education, postulated that television as a medium of communication was so geared towards entertainment that news lost any kind of seriousness and value. The focus was on filling a news program in such a way that the consumer would not switch channels. Postman argued that news had to entertain so that broadcasters could sell enough advertising to continue operating. News became entertainment just as entertainment became news.

Filtering the News

In 1976, Christian philosopher Francis Schaeffer produced a video entitled "How Should We Then Live: The Rise and Decline of Western Thought and Culture". In one fascinating scene, he illustrated how the same news story could be presented to the viewer from two completely different perspectives. Schaeffer ably demonstrated how news could be made to reflect the views of the reporter selectively presenting "facts" from a perspective that only emphasizes certain aspects of an incident.

This is particularly concerning because of reports in 2009 from Don Maclean, a former BBC Radio 2 religious program host, in which he attacked the BBC and accused it of supporting a secularist campaign "to get rid of Christianity".[12] We should not naïvely think that the news is neutral. News organizations have their own agendas and biases, whether they be making money by selecting the most captivating news items, or presenting a philosophy or political viewpoint.

Key Principles

Christianity should instill, in ever increasing measure, the quality of thoughtfulness. The Lord Jesus understood the biases of the people around him and dealt with them accordingly. The Sadducees came to him with a story about a woman who ends up marrying seven brothers. As each brother, in turn, dies, as was the Jewish practice, each succeeding brother leaves the woman to the next of kin until she herself dies. The Lord sees right through the motives behind the story and dismisses the Sadducees by quoting Scripture (Matthew 22:29–32). Like our Lord, we are to not be "fools" but "wise" recognizing that "the days are evil" (Ephesians 5:15–16).

Neither are Christians to be naïve, believing news items without questioning them and uncritically accepting the motives of the people reporting them. The Book of Proverbs has many injunctions to be wise and is very direct when it says that "The simple believes every word, but the prudent considers well his steps" (Proverbs 14:15). The apostle Paul also warns us against naïvety when he says that there are those who "do not serve our Lord Jesus Christ, but their own belly, and by smooth words and flattering speech deceive the hearts of the simple" (Romans 16:18).

Practical Advice

What does this all mean? The thing we should always remember is that the Internet is essentially unregulated. Just because a news item is posted on the Internet does not mean that it is true—be it a blog, tweet or a page from a news organization. If we are to test what the preacher says on a Sunday (1 Thessalonians 5:21, Acts 17:11), how much more should we avoid being naïve about what is posted on the Internet? We must be wise in what we see or read in the news. We must be aware of the potential bias and this may help us to analyze and think through the issues that are being presented.

This is particularly true when discussing these things in a family context. Our children will quickly pick up our views, and our biases. Particularly in their younger years, they will have a tendency to adopt these views uncritically. Even during the teenage years, when some outwardly rebel against their parents' beliefs, very few will shake off the fundamental worldview that they grew up with. The way we think, and how we react to news and information presented to us, matters a great deal. We must never forget that we live in a world of biases and agendas, in which news is seldom, if ever, presented from a Christian viewpoint.

We should also find encouragement in the way that the Internet has

Chapter 10

changed how news can now be gathered—something very different from the bleak picture that author Neil Postman presented in his book. We now have the opportunity to uncover information directly from the source, rather than simply relying on a filtered view being presented by a news agency, one that may have its own agenda. With the Internet, we can read blogs, check twitter feeds, or quickly go to another news report. This kind of access has never been possible before. It is almost as if we are now able to "cut out the middle man" from the news story. We must avoid unthinkingly accepting things, but, at the same time, we have the ability to explore news from different viewpoints. Laziness and naïvety are the great killers of objective reasoning.

Not only can we be news consumers, but we also have the opportunity to be news creators. We can use the Internet to publicize our local events, organize petitions and circulars and canvass support against anti-Christian positions. We can post sermons online, evangelistic messages, and make these available to our local community. Nothing is a substitute for the preaching of the Word, or the witness of a neighbor or of a family member. Rather, the Internet is a tool that can be used to reach people who are increasingly found at their computers. Meeting people in the time of the apostles may have meant going to the marketplace or the Acropolis. Today's communities can be found meeting on the Internet, debating ideas and getting their news and information.

We not only have access to news from around the world, we have been entrusted with the very best news of all—the good news of the gospel. We need to focus on what is achievable and develop a clear strategy for making best use of the opportunities that the World Wide Web creates. We must be proactive, not reactive.

For Discussion

Please read Acts 8:4, Acts 16:15 and Romans 3:19, 10:14–17. What opportunities does the Internet create for you and your church in your local situation, particularly when it comes to disseminating information and news, the greatest being the good news about Jesus Christ? Are there any dangers?

Please read Matthew 5:33–34, 24:26–28 and 2 Samuel 18:19–32. For many of us, the saying is true that "seeing is believing", particularly when it comes to television news. Do you think that reporting is always objective, giving every side of the story? Why are we so easily taken in and fail to comprehend the biases and, at times, anti-Christian agendas?

Notes

1 From archive.timesonline.co.uk
2 A tweet is a post or status update on Twitter, a micro-blogging service that allows messages of up to 140 characters to be shared with others
3 www.thedailybeast.com/blogs-and-stories/2009-06-14/harrowing-tweets-from-iran/
4 Quoted in www.voanews.com/english/news/middle-east/Social-Media-Playing-a-Role-in-Arab-World-Protests-114672924.html
5 www.state.gov/secretary/rm/2010/01/135519.htm
6 **E. Morozov,** *The net delusion: How not to liberate the world.* (London: Penguin, 2011)
7 The Open Society Foundations debate took place in Feb 2011. A podcast of the debate can be downloaded at fora.tv/2011/02/07/Evgeny_Morozov_The_Net_Delusion
8 www.npr.org/templates/transcript/transcript.php?storyId=126183424
9 From ABC News, available at abcnews.go.com/Technology/daily-rupert-murdoch-unveils-ipad-newspaper/story?id=12822677
10 *The Guardian,* Monday 3 October 2011
11 **Postman, N,** *Amusing ourselves to death*, Penguin Books, 1985
12 For a full report on this see the Christian Institute web page www.christian.org.uk/news/bbc-is-anti-christian-and-pro-muslim-says-ex-host

Chapter 10

Five Principles to Learn From

As we noted in the first chapter of this book, the web is the biggest media revolution since the printing press, with billions of people around the world now online. While some are brave enough to speculate on the way that the Internet is changing our society, over thirty years of experience in the Information Technology (IT) field have taught me that this is in fact almost impossible to predict. However, irrespective of what else may happen, none can deny that the Internet is here to stay. The genie is out of the bottle and there is simply no way of putting it back in. What we have seen in this book is that the Internet offers both unparalleled opportunities and very real dangers. So how do we navigate its treacherous waters? This is a very difficult question for many, particularly for parents. Yet, there are wrong ways to answer this question and right ways to approach it. The wrong ways include being prescriptive and making generalizations.

There is no expedient to which a man will not go to avoid the labor of thinking.
Thomas Edison

A prescriptive approach is one in which everything is clearly delineated as black and white in which strict "do and don't" rules can easily be laid down. While there is no denying that there are some areas, such as pornography, which we must avoid like the plague, so to speak, other areas require the careful and thoughtful application of principles, particularly those drawn from the Bible. As Thomas Edison well understood, we must think for ourselves!

We must also avoid the danger of generalization. We see a lot of this, with authors and journalists pontificating about how the Internet is changing the way we think, or how our children will grow up as a result of being exposed to computers. While we do not doubt that the

Five Principles To Learn From

technology is making a significant impact, we also need to understand that its effects on people depend on a wide range of factors, from the culture in which they grew up, to the worldview by which they live. For example, the Internet affects people in China differently from those living in the United States. In Africa, the use of payment by phone is extensive, while in the West it is, at best, very limited. Off-line browsing is prevalent in certain parts of India,[1] where the Internet may only be available for a few hours a day, while in the West, people regularly complain about not having enough bandwidth.

In these two final chapters, we will therefore aim to arrive at a considered approach—one that is based on biblical principles to pursue "whatever things are true, whatever things are noble, whatever things are just, whatever things are pure, whatever things are lovely, whatever things are of good report" (Philippians 4:8). This is going to require effort on our part to think through the kinds of issues that the Internet throws up, and to determine how to deal with them, both for our families and ourselves.

Such an approach is based on the solid foundation of biblical principles, the same kinds of principles that can still be found enshrined in the laws of most countries. These principles are also referred to as "natural law"—the law that self-evidently defines what is good and what is bad—for example, murder, theft and cheating are wrong in every society.

In this chapter we will define five key principles that we can apply to protect ourselves and our families against the worst dangers of the Internet. In the next chapter, we will conclude with five principles that can be used to make the most of the opportunities that the Internet offers. Some of these principles you will find repeated from other parts of this book. For this I make no apology, since, as any pastor or teacher knows, repetition is a key tool for instruction, one that the Lord Jesus himself used to great effect.

1. Be Realistic

For I say, through the grace given to me, to everyone who is among you, not to think of himself more highly than he ought to think, but to think soberly, as God has dealt to each one a measure of faith. (Romans 12:3)

Chapter 11

A prudent man foresees evil and hides himself; The simple pass on and are punished. (Proverbs 27:12)

Having a realistic view of our own strengths and weaknesses is not wrong, but rather something that should be encouraged. If we have a tendency to be tempted by certain things, then we need to take positive steps to avoid these. We will only know this, however, if we understand and are realistic about ourselves.

Similarly, we need to be aware of the stages that both adults and children go through. Let's not forget that we are all different and, for most people, there is such a thing as a midlife crisis, and the "terrible twos" are very real.

It is worth spending a little time on this. We need to take into account our personalities and those of our children. Children, in particular, go through various stages during their development. One of the greatest challenges of parenting is to adapt to those changes. As parents, we need to be ever aware that we generally have under twenty years to prepare our children for independent living. It is therefore critical that we understand that during this short time our children will change, and so, as they grow in maturity, we must also change the way we interact with them, as well as the way we allow them to use the Internet.

Professor Jim Renihan in his excellent book on Christian love explains that

Every adult ought to know that there is an obvious difference between the behavior of a child and a man; or at least there should be. A child is often selfish and self-centered. He speaks of himself, tries to understand life through his own experiences, reasons in simplistic fashions. Parents recognize these traits, and know that they must help their children progressively to grow out of these patterns. What is expected of a teenager is far different from a six-year-old. [2]

Even the Scriptures acknowledge this fact. "When I was a child, I spoke as a child, I understood as a child, I thought as a child; but when I became a man, I put away childish things" (1 Corinthians 13:11). While it is not

Five Principles To Learn From

the purpose of this book to explain the stages of childhood development, we need to be aware of these.

So it is that a young child thinks almost exclusively in concrete terms, and will generally accept that parents make rules. As children mature, they develop abstract thinking skills, and may go through a period of rebellion during adolescent years. As such times, parents need to focus on boundaries and principles so as to best prepare children for adulthood. During these years, children are marked by self-centeredness and a lack of self-control, with the whole world revolving around them and their friends. At the same time as pushing against parental boundaries, teenagers also want to know that the boundaries are still in place—a contradiction, I know, and something that teenagers will seldom admit to but one that provides the security that they need. There is also a feeling at this age that they know everything and that parents know nothing and don't really understand them. There is some truth in this saying: "When I was eighteen I knew everything and my father knew nothing. By the time I reached twenty-five, I was surprised how much my father had learned in the last few years."

Understanding these developmental traits will help us apply the practical advice found in this book. We may, for example, choose to limit the time that our children spend on a computer if this is getting in the way of other legitimate activities. The use of content filters should also be considered, particularly with teenagers who are seeking to break through boundaries.

Or consider the middle years. These may bring significant changes as children leave home, and job possibilities become less of a dream and more of a rut. It may be a time when we mull over those things that we never quite got around to doing. We may even find that at work younger people are being promoted instead of us. Activities may be less focused on our children. Some may find that the "glue" that held their relationship together is no longer there. This tragically leads to couples that others thought were happily married getting divorced after twenty or more years of marriage—much to everyone's surprise. There may also be a tendency during this stage to look for other things to fill the void felt when children leave home—sometimes legitimate and good things,

Chapter 11

though dangers are always close by. At this stage in life, we must be particularly wary of the temptation to form illicit relationships on the Internet. And even if they are not physical ones, any relationship that takes away the communication between husband and wife is wrong and can lead to nothing but trouble.

It should be clear to everyone that life is not a static thing. We change. Our priorities evolve, and through life we need to constantly examine ourselves (see 2 Corinthians 13:5) so as to better understand what is likely to tempt us. As we have seen in this book, much of what the Internet has to offer has both a positive and a negative side. It is not wrong to be confident about our abilities but it is wrong to overestimate them (which leads to pride), and particularly to think that we can easily turn off the computer and walk away when we are tempted by whatever sin we have a propensity towards.

Being realistic about ourselves and our families requires hard work and will not happen by accident. We should engage in the biblical practice of meditation. This is not the same as introspection. It is the careful consideration of God through his Word the Bible, and, as a result, seeing ourselves as God sees us, in realistic and reasonable terms.

I will also meditate on all Your work,
   And talk of Your deeds (Psalm 77:12).

Not only do we need to be realistic about ourselves, but we also need to understand our children and our spouse. It may seem obvious, but this means making sure that we communicate. There are a number of practical steps that we can take, such as making sure, whenever possible, that the family gathers around the dinner table, without distractions (phone, TV, etc.) and all share the events of the day. At times this will feel to parents like pulling teeth but the payoff is worth it. It may also mean having a regular family night.

Communications with teenage children can be particularly challenging and it is important that regular and natural dialog between parents and children already be in place well before the teenage years. One suggestion here is for the father, in particular, to take one of his children out for breakfast or lunch every week—on their own. Fathers do have a tendency to only communicate with their children when they are telling them off. If it is possible to begin this practice when the children are young, it will mean that regular, two-way communication between parents and children will be a natural thing and associated with the treat of breakfast or lunch. By the time the children reach their teenage years, communication channels will already be open and natural.

2. Be Disciplined

Lack of self-control is reaching epidemic proportions in our society. According to Webster's dictionary, self-control is the ability to exhibit "control of one's self; restraint exercised over one's self." Yet we are constantly bombarded with encouragements to indulge ourselves "because you are worth it", to quote one well-known advertising slogan. This lack of self-control, or discipline, is having huge societal impacts, whether it is the binge drink culture, the growth of obesity or many other problems. According to one study,

> Scientists found that preschool-age children who had trouble with self-control and the ability to delay gratification gained more weight by the time they were preteens than those who were better at regulating their behavior ... of the 805 children in the study, 47% had trouble with self-restraint.[3]

Lack of restraint is found everywhere, whether in eating, drinking, sexual activity, anger, or any number of activities. However, it should be the goal of all people to cultivate in themselves, and in their children, self-discipline. Not doing this can lead to disaster in the Internet age where everything is available online. Doing things to excess should have no place in our lives and in our families.

The Scriptures are overflowing with injunctions to be disciplined and self-controlled. Yet, we seldom hear any sermons on the subject. This is not just moralizing! Self-control is listed as being the "fruit of the Spirit" in Galatians 5:23, that is, a quality that should mark a Christian apart; a trait that is deepened and that grows with Christian maturity as the Spirit of God himself works in the life of a believer.

Chapter 11

In contrast, in a passage that would not be amiss in any of today's newspapers, the apostle Paul predicts that "in the last days" (that is the time that we live in), "men will be lovers of themselves, lovers of money, boasters, proud, blasphemers, disobedient to parents, unthankful, unholy, unloving, unforgiving, slanderers, *without self-control*, brutal, despisers of good, traitors, headstrong, haughty, lovers of pleasure rather than lovers of God, having a form of godliness but denying its power" (2 Timothy 3:2–5, my italics).

We could go on looking at examples from our society, as well as from history, though this problem is self evident to anyone today. We have already seen in this book that lack of self-control, when it comes to the Internet, can lead to all kinds of trouble, from the inability to stop ourselves wandering onto undesirable websites, to posting pictures or messages in the heat of the moment that later come back to haunt us.

3. Be Prepared

The Bible never pretends that developing the character required to live a moral and godly life is easy. It speaks of us as engaged in constant battle and often uses illustrations from sport or the battlefield:

> Therefore I run thus: not with uncertainty. Thus I fight: not as one who beats the air. But I discipline my body and bring it into subjection, lest, when I have preached to others, I myself should become disqualified (1 Corinthians 9:26–27).

Christians are not couch potatoes, settled down in the sofa of ease, consuming scraps of food fed to them by online preachers and unable to move themselves to reach for the keyboard to change to a different website. They should be disciplined and they should be prepared. The athlete who runs a marathon does not simply turn up on the day of the race and expect to win without having first undergone months or, in many instances, years of training.

The verses quoted above speak of discipline and of bringing our bodies into subjection. It is hard work but it is exactly what is needed when facing any form of temptation. If we are not prepared; if we have not trained our minds and our thoughts; if we have not sought to immerse

Five Principles To Learn From

ourselves in Scripture bathed with prayer, then we will fall prey to the first temptation that winds its way to us through cyberspace.

Being prepared will mean limiting our time on the Internet so that we have time to study Scripture, go to church, pray, meet with others, take part in Christian activities and to learn, grow and flourish.

Being prepared will mean that we will be aware of our weaknesses, so much so that for us, avoiding certain types of websites or even the Internet altogether may be the only reasonable approach.

Being prepared will give us the insights we need to better understand when the Internet is beginning to dominate our spare time and becoming an addiction and when we should walk away and take a break.

4. Be Structured

"To everything there is a season, a time for every purpose under heaven ..." (Ecclesiastes 3:1)

A close companion to self-discipline is the idea of structure, something that is particularly helpful for families. The example of setting aside an evening a week for family time requires structure. But if we do this, we will find ways of using the Internet in a positive and constructive manner. However, this cannot happen without structure and discipline.

Similarly, having a "phones on the fridge" policy, where all members of the family put their mobile devices on the fridge for a specific event such as the evening meal, can be highly beneficial. It is tragic to see families not spending time together, but rather racing between activities, "chatting" to friends online or just watching television. We need time together to discuss what happened during the day and share issues and problems. But it won't work without structure and this requires consistency. A "phones on the fridge" policy will never work if the parents jump up from the dinner table to pick up that important text or email that has been expected from the office. We all need to be consistent.

In Scripture, we even see the Lord Jesus setting time aside for particular activities, and structuring his day accordingly. At one point, he had to send the crowds away and spend time by himself going "to the mountain to pray" (Mark 6:46).

Being structured will help us avoid the danger of time wasting—a

Chapter 11

pernicious evil. We certainly need time to rest and relax. We are made to work for six days a week and to rest on the seventh. That is why "the Sabbath was made for man, and not man for the Sabbath" (Mark 2:27). That is also why it is necessary to take time off during the year to "recharge our batteries".

But, if we are honest with ourselves, we will have to admit that we are easily prone to time-wasting and that the Internet can have a tendency to draw us in sometimes for hours at a time. We need to consider the use of our time. It may seem obvious, but an hour just spent browsing the Internet is an hour that we will never get back. To help us redeem the time, we need to constantly challenge ourselves about our use of time. If you knew that this hour was your last hour of life, would you want to spend it browsing the Internet?

5. Be Informed

"Behold, I send you out as sheep in the midst of wolves. Therefore be wise as serpents and harmless as doves" (Matthew 10:16).

The fifth principle in this section is so important that it should become part of our DNA. Whenever we go to any new website, our first thought should be to ask ourselves how the owners of the site make their money. This is not simply a cynical view, but rather a realistic one. At the very least, programming, servicing and maintaining a website costs money. The old adages hold true: "There is no such thing as a free lunch (or a free website)", and, "If it sounds too good to be true it probably is." We need to remember the saying that "if it's free, then you are the product".

The motivation behind commerce in the West became all too apparent during the financial crisis of the first part of the twenty-first century. What many have said and known for a long time became clear: our society revolves around greed and selfishness. Software companies such as Yahoo, Bing, Google or Facebook may appear to offer free services, but they still manage to make billions of dollars of profit by selling information about us to advertisers and helping companies to target us via the Internet.

That is not to say that we should not use the Internet or use any other form of media. Rather, we must take a close look at any website, and make sure that we are informed about what motivates the site owners. Usually, it will be some form of profit motivation. I am by no means suggesting that there is a moral imperative against making a profit. In fact, in the parable of the talents (Matthew 25:14–30) the servants were commended for being good stewards and investing wisely so as to return a profit. It is right that we should know about the benefits of a website but we also need to be aware of the motivations of the site owners. Sometimes, not everything is what it seems. The Internet not only offers opportunities to spread the good news of the gospel, it also allows all kinds of tricksters to peddle their trade on a global scale. Let's therefore be informed, and always be cautious.

Notes

1 For an interesting article on how entrepreneurs in India are using SMS technology to expand the reach of the Internet see—
www.npr.org/blogs/alltechconsidered/2011/01/03/132236616/no-facebook-in-india-mobile-users-have-another-option#more

2 **James M Renihan,** *True Love—understanding the real meaning of Christian love* (2010, EP Books)

3 Quoted in *Time Magazine* and available online at
www.time.com/time/health/article/0,8599,1889942,00.html

Chapter 12

Five Principles to Run With

The marketplace in Ephesus where the apostle Paul would have preached

While it is essential to be aware of some of the dangers of the Internet, we also need to grasp its benefits. As we have already seen, the Internet is here to stay. Its arrival has introduced deep changes in our society both in how we relate to one another and the way we communicate. These changes are so significant that we can rightly compare the era we are living in with the Industrial Revolution.

While there are still dangers, many of which we have considered in this book, there are also significant opportunities. It is always easier to look at something like the Internet and condemn it out of hand without thinking about the good that we can achieve through its judicious use. Rather, we should consider the Internet to be just like a tool, a powerful and sophisticated one, but a tool nonetheless. This tool can be used to demolish, hurt and tear down, or it can be used to build the most amazing things. The key is not so much in the tool itself but rather in the hands that wield it. That is one of the reasons why in this book we have sought to demystify the Internet, to present it as just a very fast and powerful communications system. Like the clay spoken of by the apostle Paul, by the grace of God, it can be used as a vessel of honor or dishonor (see Romans 9:21).

In this final chapter, we will aim to get beyond the prejudices and fears that typically blight the new and the unknown, and think positively and rationally about how to grasp the opportunities that the Internet presents. I hope that, by doing this, we can be amazed by what, with the Lord's help, can be achieved.

1. Be Real

But let your 'Yes' be 'Yes,' and your 'No,' 'No.' For whatever is more than these is from the evil one (Matthew 5:37).

As we have seen, the Internet and, in particular, social media, create the possibility of our projecting a different persona than the one we really have. We all have heard of comedians mocking dating agencies where, on a first date, a person turns up to find that the other party looks nothing like the picture they saw. On the Internet, it is very easy to pretend to be somebody else—either consciously or subconsciously.

But if we turn this on its head, we will see that the Internet creates the opportunity for us to be exactly who we are—no more and no less—and to meet and interact with others around the world. We should not be ashamed of who we are and how God made us, our interests and our passions—as long as these are legitimate and not evil, of course. The Internet allows us to meet and discuss things with others who share the same interests or perhaps have experienced similar situations.

There are, for example, thousands of support groups, ranging from groups for cancer patients and Huntingdon's disease, to groups helping children with Downs Syndrome. According to one expert, "More than any other segment of our society, those people [with rare diseases] are tremendously helped by the Internet."[1]

The Internet allows us to build friendships with people of similar interests or to find support. We must recognize that these kinds of relationships are often different from the ones we may have with people we meet face to face. But Internet relationships are, nonetheless real, even though we must be realistic about what they are and what they are not.

The cardinal sin, however, is pretending to be someone else. The Lord Jesus constantly condemned hypocrisy. To reiterate the point made earlier, the word itself derives from the ancient Greek *hypokrisis*—a stage actor playing a part, and usually wearing a mask so as to better

Chapter 12

pretend to be someone else. There is little doubt that the Internet has created an atmosphere of *hypokrisis*.

In contrast, we must be straightforward. We are who we are, and should not be ashamed of this. We befriend people, share interests with others and join groups online, realizing the dangers, but also the benefits, and never pretending to be something that we are not.

2. Be Opportunistic

The Internet opens a large range of opportunities. For example, if we have a particular interest in a country, maybe one to which our church has sent out missionaries, we can easily find out a vast amount of information online about the country they are working in. We can be informed on the political and cultural situation and build up an understanding that will help us better support and pray for them.

Or perhaps we are trying to help someone in a difficult situation and feel at a loss to know what to say. The Internet contains vast sources of help. There is help for parents, help for the bereaved, help for those seeking information about Christianity, etc. There are good sites and there are also bad sites. There is no reason, however, why a church or a denomination should not be able to point people to the good sites. It will require a little research, but will be well worth it. For example, sites like Sermon Audio[2] carry hundreds of thousands of helpful biblical Christian sermons. They can be searched by speaker or by topic. There are Bibles online[3], hymns[4], books, sermons, videos online. These are all resources that can be used.

For those involved in running a youth club in a church or preparing for Vacation Bible School, there are vast amounts of resources available online to help, from craft ideas to songs and talks. Some are free of charge while others charge a small fee.

For some, the opportunities will come in the form of sharing, creating a blog, posting some sermons, or even tweeting about an event. The Internet provides us with a means of getting our message out. After all, why should the forces of evil be the only ones to use the Internet to communicate when we have a much greater, more majestic and so much more important message of our own?

Five Principles To Run With

We need to be opportunistic and use the resources that are available to us for good. While others have focused on the evil that comes from abuse and the dark side of what is available on the Internet, there is also a positive side, an opportunity to share, to be a light shining on a hill (Matthew 5:14–16).

3. Be Involved

Therefore comfort each other and edify one another, just as you also are doing (1 Thessalonians 5:11).

I grew up in a missionary family—a missionary kid as we are affectionately called. My parents were missionaries in France, a country in which I was born and grew up. Every year or two, the family returned for a few days to my parents' sending church in Northern Ireland. As a child, I knew little about this church, except that I was expected to stand at the front and "say a few words in French". I did not get to know any of the other children in the church, and they did not know me.

Today, the story could (and should) be very different. There is now no reason why a sending church cannot keep in touch regularly with its missionaries, whether through Skype, email, Facebook or any number of other media. There is even the opportunity to have the missionaries report from time to time at a church meeting over Skype while still in location. Or why not encourage families in the church to set aside a little time every month with their children to look at what is happening in the part of world that church missionaries are living in? They can even use Facebook to keep in touch. Young people in the church can easily keep in touch with their peers on the mission field. There is little doubt that if I was growing up as a missionary kid today, this kind of communication would have made a world of difference to me. I would have known something about the sending church, would have had regular contact, and may even have been "friends" with some of the young people, sharing pictures, stories and information.

The Internet can make a huge difference to those in isolated or just in different situations. But it requires us to keep in touch, to get involved. It will take effort, but it will be worth it.

We need also to be involved with one another in a local church

Chapter 12

situation. One of the easiest places to hide and to be lonely is in a large church surrounded by others that we know little about. We need to get involved, know about each other, and be prepared to hold ourselves accountable to others because, as we have seen, the Internet brings with it an abundance of dangers. Remember that the local church is a great place to seek out people to whom we can make ourselves accountable. The Bible repeatably urges us to encourage others and to hold each other accountable:

> But exhort one another daily, while it is called "Today," lest any of you be hardened through the deceitfulness of sin (Hebrews 3:13, see also Titus 2:1–8).

We are accountable, first to God (Romans 14:12), then to one another. Sadly, this is not a principle that is emphasized enough. Our society promotes the freedom of the individual, while a true biblical view sees our freedom in a different light—one that, this side of heaven, still requires accountability.

In previous chapters we noted the use of accountability software such as Covenant Eyes and X3Watch.[5] All of these require an agreement between people to hold each other accountable. It requires openness as well as a willingness to get involved. Our lives are often complicated and messy. They are filled with issues, problems, joys, temptations and victories. Let's be involved—it's the right thing to do.

4. Be Converted

This may seem like a strange thing to say in a chapter that is supposed to deal with principles that will help us to deal with Internet-related issues. Yet, what we have seen is that the Internet has a dark side, dangers that need to be avoided. We have also seen that our very natures are such that we have a propensity to be tempted by the seedier and baser aspects of the Internet—and this is the whole point of making ourselves accountable. When we yield to that temptation, we sin. Our sin is not just against ourselves, or others, but, most importantly, it is a breaking of the Law given by the Creator of heaven and earth, God himself.

One of the greatest antidotes to falling into sin is to pray about what

Five Principles To Run With

we are about to do before we do it. But to do this, we need to have a relationship with the God to whom we are praying.

Throughout this book, we have advocated values that are unashamedly Christian in nature. They are also built into us as human beings (our consciences) and by God's goodness we have also been given some means (sometimes referred to as common grace) by which we can resist the temptations. But we all have to admit that we do fall short of perfection.

The difference between the converted Christian believer and the unbeliever is that when a Christian falls, that person can pray for forgiveness from God and know that all his or her sins are covered by the life, death and resurrection of the Lord Jesus Christ. In a time of need, Christians can also pray to receive strength from the Holy Spirit, who is God himself living in them.

If you, however, are not a believer, if you have not come to God on your knees asking for forgiveness for your sins and trusting in the Lord Jesus Christ, you have none of this. You may see yourself accurately, with your strengths and weaknesses, and, if you do, you will know that you are far from perfect. God requires the perfection of Jesus Christ to cover you, not just now, but for all of eternity. Often, the older we get, the more we try to hide from the reality of eternity that lies ahead of us, though we are increasingly acutely aware of the brevity and seeming pointlessness of our lives. We are born, go to school and maybe university, and then spend the rest of our lives working to make ends meet, perhaps at the same time raising a family. Before we know it, time has flown past us, we look back and wonder where it has gone, and still try to hide from what lies ahead. Maybe we have found a little entertainment and maybe even some purpose in what the Internet has to offer, but it is all a vapor, just a passing shadow, very like those inscriptions found on gravestones—a sentence to sum up our lives, and soon even those will be weather worn and hard to read.

In just a few years, we will also be like the people buried under those gravestones with others walking past and wondering what we were like, the flowers on the gravestone long since gone, and the grave unattended. Some enterprising people are trying very hard to provide a degree of

Chapter 12

longevity by offering to imprint 3D barcodes on a gravestone. When scanned, the bar code will take you to a webpage where images, stories and videos of the deceased are to be found. But this, as interesting as it is, is still just a shadow, a chasing after wind.

What we need, both now and for eternity, is the God of eternity, the God of love, the One who will always be with us (Matthew 28:20) and will help us in our time of need (Hebrews 4:16). There is no greater antidote to temptation, whether on the Internet or elsewhere. Every Christian principle we have advocated in this book stems from God himself through the death of the Lord Jesus Christ. With Jesus as our Savior, our lives will be totally bathed in his love, our outlook will be revolutionized and we will find a real family and community in the church well beyond the loose relationships that we can form on social networks. With so much available at the press of a few keys, so much tempting us, so much pulling us in all kinds of directions, there has never been a time when it is more important to trust the Solid Rock who is Jesus Christ:

> For God so loved the world that He gave His only begotten Son, that whoever believes in Him should not perish but have everlasting life. For God did not send His Son into the world to condemn the world, but that the world through Him might be saved (John 3:16–17).

5. Be Ready to Think Big

The picture at the beginning of this chapter is one of Ephesus, a site that I visited recently. I was not only impressed by the size and details of the excavation, but was also reminded of the story of the apostle Paul coming to this great ancient City.[6] There, in front of me, was the amphitheater where the citizens of Ephesus cried out for two hours, "Great is Diana of the Ephesians!" and next to it is the marketplace where Paul preached. Paul was a man who thought big. He was not afraid to trust God and take on challenges that others would have considered impossible. The missionary William Carey was a similar man. Before he went out to India in 1793, he preached a remarkable sermon entitled "Expect great things from God! Attempt great things for God!" He knew that, with God, nothing is impossible.

Five Principles To Run With

The amphitheater in Ephesus

Paul, the great apostle to the Gentiles, did not simply set off on his missionary journeys without first devising a clear strategy: he would generally travel to key cities and locations (Corinth, Ephesus, etc.), then search out people who already had an interest in God as he had revealed himself in the Old Testament (such as those found in Synagogues or at a prayer meeting, as in the case of Lydia). Finally, after preaching to these people, he would usually branch out to others in the area. He had a clear strategy to make the most of the opportunities that he had. In many ways, the time in which Paul ministered was a remarkable one, with well maintained and paved Roman roads connecting the major cities of the Roman empire, common languages widely spoken, and a dispersed and widely established Jewish community. The apostle Paul used all of these new means of communication and even used his privileges as a Roman Citizen when it became necessary (Acts 25:11).

Today, we live in a similar time of opportunity, one in which we can reach much of the human population using the Internet. If the apostle Paul had lived in our day, what would he have done? He would surely have assessed the opportunities open to him to use the Internet. Although the

Chapter 12

Internet can never be a substitute for the preaching of the Word, the witness of a neighbor or that of a family member and the local church, it is nonetheless a tool that can be used to reach people who are increasingly found surfing on their computers, tablets and Smartphones. Meeting people in the time of the apostles may have meant going to the marketplace or the Acropolis, but today communities can be found meeting on the Internet, debating ideas, getting their news and information.

If Paul used the resources at his disposal, so should we. Think of the Roman road system creating an unparalleled opportunity to carry the gospel to the whole known world. With the Internet, we have a much more extensive and immediate network of connections. We have been entrusted with the very best news of all—the good news about Jesus Christ. We need to grasp every opportunity, develop clear strategies in our churches, and focus on what is achievable. So much is possible that it would be disastrous and very wrong to ignore the opportunities that the World Wide Web creates. We must be proactive rather than reactive. The Internet is a tool, but the message is what we need to communicate. We are not all pioneers, but we are all called upon to make the most of every opportunity that is presented to us. We have a great and wondrous God from whom we can "expect great things". For such an amazing Savior, nothing should be able to stop us from attempting "great things for God"! After all, what would Paul have done?

Notes

1. **Mary Dunkle,** Communications Vice President for the National Organization for Rare Disorders (NORD). Quoted in www.medicinenet.com/script/main/art.asp?articlekey=126476
2. www.sermonaudio.com
3. This book's publisher—Day One Publications—points authors in their style guide to the online website www.biblegateway.com. There are also other sites.
4. I have been involved for a number of years with a British hymnbook—*Christian Hymns* www.christianhymns.org.uk. There is an associated website that provides words and music for many of these hymns, as well as new tunes for old hymns—wwww.ihymns.org
5. www.x3watch.com
6. See Acts 19 for the story of this missionary journey.

About Day One:

Day One's threefold commitment:

- To be faithful to the Bible, God's inerrant, infallible Word;
- To be relevant to our modern generation;
- To be excellent in our publication standards.

I continue to be thankful for the publications of Day One. They are biblical; they have sound theology; and they are relative to the issues at hand. The material is condensed and manageable while, at the same time, being complete—a challenging balance to find. We are happy in our ministry to make use of these excellent publications.

JOHN MACARTHUR, PASTOR-TEACHER, GRACE COMMUNITY CHURCH, CALIFORNIA

It is a great encouragement to see Day One making such excellent progress. Their publications are always biblical, accessible and attractively produced, with no compromise on quality. Long may their progress continue and increase!

JOHN BLANCHARD, AUTHOR, EVANGELIST AND APOLOGIST

Visit our web site for more information and to request a free catalogue of our books.

www.dayone.co.uk

**Family Money Matters:
How to run your family finances
to God's glory**

JOHN TEMPLE

112PP, ILLUSTRATED PAPERBACK

ISBN 978–1–84625–203–7

How we manage our family finances is always an important issue, but is particularly topical given the West's financial crisis. As Christians, our lives should demonstrate different values from those of the world around us, so what should our financial priorities be? How should we plan financially for the future? Should we ever get into debt? In this thoroughly practical book designed for the layperson, John Temple describes the secular economic order of the Western world and then establishes biblical principles of home finance. Practical advice in areas such as debt, choosing a home, buying a car, insurance, and pensions, is supplemented by tables and downloadable spreadsheets.

'I am thankful for Temple's book. Here is a man who loves God, loves the wisdom of the Word and is zealous to help you build a biblical worldview of your money and how you use it. What is even better is that he will not only challenge the motives of your heart and tell you how to think, he will also tell you what to do.'
PAUL DAVID TRIPP, AUTHOR OF AGE OF OPPORTUNITY